SOCIAL POLICY IN DEVELOPING COUNTRIES

ARTHUR LIVINGSTONE

Volume 90

Routledge
Taylor & Francis Group
LONDON AND NEW YORK

First published in 1969

This edition first published in 2011
by Routledge
2 Park Square, Milton Park, Abingdon, Oxon, OX14 4RN

Simultaneously published in the USA and Canada
by Routledge

711 Third Avenue, New York, NY 10017

Routledge is an imprint of the Taylor & Francis Group, an informa business

First issued in paperback 2013

British Library Cataloguing in Publication Data
A catalogue record for this book is available from the British Library

ISBN 13: 978-0-415-58414-2 (Set)
eISBN 13: 978-0-203-84035-1 (Set)
ISBN 13: 978-0-415-60185-6 (Volume 90 hbk)
eISBN 13: 978-0-203-83552-4 (Volume 90)
ISBN 13: 978-0-415-85074-2 (Volume 90 pbk)

Publisher's Note
The publisher has gone to great lengths to ensure the quality of this reprint but points out that some imperfections in the original copies may be apparent.

Disclaimer
The publisher has made every effort to trace copyright holders and welcomes correspondence from those they have been unable to contact.

Social Policy in Developing Countries

by Arthur Livingstone
Department of Overseas Administrative Studies
University of Manchester

LONDON
ROUTLEDGE & KEGAN PAUL
NEW YORK : HUMANITIES PRESS

First published 1969
by Routledge & Kegan Paul Ltd
Broadway House, 68-74 Carter Lane
London, E.C.4

SBN 7100 6442 X (C)
SBN 7100 6443 8 (P)

General editor's introduction

The study of social policy developed in the industrialized countries of the Western world and inevitably, the new techniques of study have been applied first in the societies where they have been developed; but there is a tendency to assume that social policy is concerned with the problems of the Welfare State, and stops at its frontiers. We study the 'shortage of doctors' in the United States, which has one medical practitioner to about 730 inhabitants, but not in Mali, which has one to 77,000. We become angry about child poverty in Britain, where at least no family starves, while Indian or Biafran children die by the thousand.

In most of Africa, most of Asia, the Middle East and parts of Central and South America, the diet is minimal, the increase of population is high, the average expectation of life is low, the majority of the adult population is illiterate. Yet this group of countries, comprising 85 per cent of the world's population, has something like 10 per cent of the world's income, and 5 per cent of its scientific resources. Can we even begin to discuss the problems of the redistribution of wealth without concerning ourselves with this massive and tragic example of inequality?

Gunnar Myrdal[1] suggested that the democratic Welfare States of the West are inherently protectionist and nationalistic, and put the case for international study and international concern bluntly as a matter not only of social morality but of expediency.

The only answer is to go 'beyond the Welfare State' to the Welfare World. The transfer of money and resources by governmental and non-governmental agencies, though valuable and urgently needed, is not much more than 'rosewater on a volcano' to use Reinhold Niebuhr's vivid phrase. And the effects have been at least partly negated by the brain-drain. Professor Titmuss suggests that

> . . . since 1949, the United States has absorbed (and to some extent deliberately recruited) the import of 100,000 doctors, scientists and engineers . . . in about eighteen years, the United States will have saved some $4,000 million by not having to educate and train, or train fully, this vasty quantity of human capital . . . estimates have been made that this foreign aid to America is as great, or greater, than the total of American aid to countries abroad since 1949.[2]

'Human beings' writes Mr. Livingstone, 'are vital economic resources.' The training of human beings in an understanding of the issues of social policy is basic to development, because the ends of development are social ends.

> If you give a man a fish, he will eat once
> If you teach a man to fish, he will eat for the rest of his life.
> If you are thinking a year ahead, sow seed.
> If you are thinking ten years ahead, plant a tree.
> If you are thinking a hundred years ahead, educate the people.
> By sowing seed, you will harvest once.
> By planting a tree, you will harvest tenfold.
> By educating the people, you will harvest one hundredfold.[3]

[1] G. Myrdal, *Beyond the Welfare State*, University Paperbacks Edition, 1960, p. 164.

[2] R. M. Titmuss, *Commitment to Welfare*, Unwin University Books, 1968, p. 126.

[3] Kuan-tsu. (4th-3rd century B.C.)

Contents

1
Introduction

In Islamic teaching one instruction forbids the devout Moslem to sleep in peace if at sundown there exists one hungry person within his range of vision. Other religions lay a similar personal and social obligation on their adherents. Taken literally, throughout the world, this observance would induce a chronic insomnia of epidemic proportions. Periodically, dramatic news headlines describe widespread starvation in countries beset by famine and other calamities. As serious, if not more so, is the constant condition of millions of the earth's inhabitants where the insidious effects of prolonged malnutrition and untreated sickness leave them only a half life within the brain. The consequences, in terms of human debility and apathy, are as significant for the prospects of national development as they are tragic for the personal destinies of over two thousand million people living now in under-developed countries—70% of the human race.

The lack of any educational opportunity for many millions of people, and probably for their children's children, heightens their already perilous condition. There exist to-day more than seven hundred million adult illiterates, representing about half of the world adult population, a deprived group whose numbers are increasing every year. Taking one of the most extreme contrasts given in the Overseas Development Institute Publication, *World III*

(Macmillan, 1964): In 1960, 9% of the Sudanese school-age population was enrolled in primary and secondary schools, compared with 80-81% in the U.K. and the U.S.A., enrolment in higher education at that time was thirty-four per one hundred thousand of population in the Sudan, compared with four hundred and two in the U.K. and one thousand nine hundred and eighty-three in the U.S.A.

This is only part of the problem; millions more suffer a brief and irrelevant education that provides little hope of personal advancement or a contribution to the development of their country. In rural areas they are found working in penurious and non-progressive agricultural occupations; in cities and towns they crowd in shanty fringes seeking the regular cash wages in industry and commerce. In many cases, over-population imposes an unbearable strain on countries with slender resources of material wealth and technical competence; sometimes a country is too small in geographical area and population ever to provide a viable economic unit. The future discovery of oil deposits or some such miracle may be the dream that holds at bay an annihilating sense of despair. Large or small, the developing countries contain that half of the world's population which earns only 7% of the world's income; a quarter of the world population, found in Europe and North America earns nearly three-quarters of the world's income (Macmillan, 1964).

A number of other indigenous factors may aggravate a state of endemic poverty: political instability and capricious political leadership; rigid social classifications and economic disparities; traditional attitudes inducing inertia and resistance to change and modernization; destructive civil or extra-territorial warfare; catastrophes of flood, earthquake and drought. As general information, most of this depressing picture is known to people throughout the world who read newspapers, listen to the radio and watch television, and travel outside the modern watering places. To understand the full implications of the problem, both for those who suffer from it and for those outside it, something more is necessary than the grim evidence of statistics and eye-witness reports of human suffering. Acknowledging the risks that attend the generalization of such a wide range of problems, with a possible over-simplification of the issues involved, it is important to look more closely at conditions which create for many millions of people in the world today an inescapable human predicament. Basically the predicament is the hopelessness of the man and the family caught in a net of poverty, ignorance and disease. In the industrialized countries, whatever the memories of the economic depression of the second quarter of this century, however bitter the experience of destructive wars, despite the hazards represented by the recurrent financial crises of the present day, such societies are not only becoming increasingly affluent but offer rich rewards for the application of intelligence and personal industry. In many other countries, as they are politically, culturally and economically conditioned today, the human attributes of hard work, thrift, imagination, and perseverance have only limited relevance to either the problems endemic to the society or to the measures required to solve them.

The greater part of the population of Asian, African, Middle Eastern and South American countries are engaged in agricultural work, sometimes as many as 90% of the people in any one country. In the 1950's, India, Thailand and the Sudan (to quote only three countries of many with similar conditions) had between 70% and 90% of their total population dependent on agriculture, compared with 3% in the U.K. and 13% in the U.S.A. (Moyes & Hayter, 1964). So often this agricultural work is an unrelenting struggle for mere survival, but even then survival only to an age which in most developed countries represents the early years of a personal career. For the peasant-owner, renter, or neo serf of his land, the struggle is against many enemies of the body and of the soul: barren soil, fragmented land ownings, landlord despotism, crippling indebtedness to the money lender, the devastation of drought and flood, archaic farm equipment, primitive methods of transport and communication, inadequate markets, lack of either formal education or technical skills, and, overall, no expectation for oneself or one's children of being able to reach beyond the harsh and repetitive toil that brings no increase in the products of the land or the fortunes of the family.

From this catalogue of human woes there might easily emerge the outline of an agricultural man who was largely an automaton, moving in a zombie-like trance through the vicissitudes that assail him from every side. This is far from the truth. Rural peoples in very impoverished circumstances live by a rich store of legend and tradition. Family and community life is enlivened by the festivals that mark the significant events in their personal and group associations. A pervasive tang of humour may be only faintly discernible to the outsider. That which is so often exasperating to the activist—the apathy, the sense of resignation to the inevitable, the resistance to change—is the product of generations of last ditch battles with an implacable environment and the interior weaknesses of ignorance and a lack of hope. Against such a background, exhortations on the fruits of hard work, thrift and co-operation are met with the cynicism they no doubt deserve. Both the social and the technological barriers to real change are formidable indeed. Despite decades of effort and some encouraging achievements, few governments, or the international organizations advising them, have been able to develop a progressive agricultural economy. Typical of comparable figures for other kinds of agricultural products is the 1961-2 contrast between the annual wheat yield in developing countries (an average of 7 cwt. an acre) and that of other countries (28 cwt. an acre in the U.K., 33 cwt. an acre in Denmark). Not the least problem for governments in low income countries is the recognition that agricultural development is an international as well as a domestic issue for them, bound up with the readiness of other countries to accord them favourable terms of trade, and with the availability of international loans at interest rates that do not cripple the country's rate of progress.

In the present decade we have become familiar with the recurrent warnings of the Food and Agricultural Organization and other international bodies about deteriorating food supplies in, or for, low income countries, the constant threat of famine in some regions, and the general inability to find a remedy for the increasing gap between the rate of economic and social development in the more affluent nations and that achieved by countries which carry the greater proportion of the world's population. Obviously, the problem is wider than that concerned with agricultural production. But in most developing countries a high proportion of the national product, and of the working population, is related to agriculture. All the more imperative that increased attention be given to a domestic and international problem that continues to baffle us.

In developing countries, as in most other parts of the world, cities and towns are attracting people from villages and farms, drawn by the prospects of regular work and cash wages. Large numbers of these migrants are men who come alone, arranging for part of their wages to be sent regularly to the rural families they have left behind. Many will return home at least once a year, at harvest time. Alone or with families they will live for most of the year in makeshift dwellings on the edge of the towns or cities, frequently without fresh water supplies or sanitary provisions, and almost certainly with no access to competent medical care or to regular education for their children. A sobering reflection that these plague-risk slums and the menial jobs of their occupants are by them thought preferable to what they left behind in the rural areas.

A large influx of rural people to urban areas produces an insupportable burden for both the individual and the country as a whole. Some years ago, as part of a national industrial development plan, one government in a country of nearly 50 million people sought to attract rural dwellers for factory work in the capital city. Contracts were arranged for nine months' employment periods to the industry, the other three months to be spent at home during the crucial part of the agricultural year. Concrete cubicles were erected in the city to accommodate the male workers who would spend the nine months' period separated from their families. The scheme had been implemented only a short while before many disturbing habits and attitudes became evident among a considerable section of the work group. Chronic absenteeism, alcoholism (in a country with legal prohibition), delinquency, venereal disease, mental illness—these were the more dramatic forms of a general malaise amongst these new industrial workers. Production broke down, and the Government hurried to establish a Committee of Inquiry. There was nothing startlingly novel about its findings but they were of important significance for this and other occasions where people are moved from one sub-culture to another. Separation from the carefully defined relationships of an extended family system in a rural society; accommodation in the intimidating bleakness of a concrete cubicle; the demands of an unfamiliar repetitive task for several hours a day without interruption; a regular acquisition of money with so many incitements to spend it and so few of the traditional restraints to curb the spendthrift: these were the experiences to engender loneliness and a personal disorientation. A broad range of issues concerned with the social consequences of technological change is to be found in a University of Dacca Survey (*Human and Social Impact*, etc., 1956).

This then is the human situation in many countries, of many millions of population: rural families eking out an existence that seems not far removed from that of the cave dweller; urban inhabitants whose work is so often trivial, parasitic. Such people, and their governments, are caught in a familiar vicious circle. They lack the national resources to provide jobs with adequate wages and prospects for the future, houses that offer space and dignity in personal living, educational facilities for children both in the appreciation of knowledge and the development of technical skills, health services that can bring children into the world potentially fit for a full and vigorous life. Without these economic and social achievements, a country cannot hope to improve its levels of living. Human beings are vital economic resources. They are both the ends and the means of national planning. Where crippled mentally, physically and emotionally, they provide a stubborn obstacle to the fulfilment of even the most imaginative plans for national development. The dimensions of this obstacle, and what might be done to remove it, can perhaps better be understood by looking at three major human needs in impoverished countries—education, health, and social welfare. These three areas of need do not represent the sum of individual or national requirements but they mirror both the nature of the distress and what hope exists of relieving it.

2
Education

In many countries whose poverty and general underdevelopment is the subject of this examination, there is a curious ambivalence towards education and the educator. Along with an almost obsessive striving for the status that education can offer goes a resistance to the application of knowledge in circumstances where it is most desperately needed. In some developing countries, the resistance to technological innovation may come not from the unenlightened peasantry but from an educated élite who fear its threat to an established way of life. One Secretary of Education, administratively responsible for the schools programme of millions of children in a subsistence economy, resolutely held out for years against the inclusion of technical subjects in the curricula. Often there is veneration of the sage with a repudiation of the influence his wisdom represents. Students reading their own public odes to some philosopher-father may be members of a clandestine group dedicated to deposing him. To attach semantic labels such as hypocrisy or insincerity to those attitudes and behaviour patterns is over-simplification, a superficial reading of what is at stake. One of the central issues for a society is the particular kind of value it places on knowledge and its application to assisting human need. It is at this point that we may encounter some of the most frustrating impediments to social progress.

It seems obvious that if a country is to acquire the accumulation of knowledge necessary for integrated development there must be a social climate favourable to two types of human activity. First, exercise of the free rein of the imagination in searching for and experimenting with new ideas; secondly, the participation of people at all educational and economic levels in the quest for increased knowledge and skill. In many parts of the world one or both of these prerequisites are absent. The nature of certain traditions, economic structures, and political systems stifle the inducement to individual enterprise and the capacity for innovation. Such restrictive influences represent one of the major obstacles to social development.

Continuously, every society is confronted with the problem of balancing permissiveness for individual expression with the social obligations binding on a person as a member of a group. This issue has particular urgency for under-developed countries. Their need for entrepreneurs is paramount in every vocational and commercial field. The slow development of entrepreneurial activity in many countries stems from many limiting circumstances, most of them understandable and, in the near future, not easily reducible. One serious limitation is a social structure that does not readily permit change. Traditional attitudes and practices, whether based on religious beliefs or largely on the sanctity of custom, can frustrate the assimilation of new knowledge and its application to the urgencies of economic and social need. Both international consultants and indigenous leaders working with technical assistance programmes know how arduous and slow-moving is the task of introducing unfamiliar concepts and techniques to a society which must appropriate them if it is to progress but may believe itself to be threatened with cultural disintegration by accepting 'modern' ideas and methods. This can be a problem at any level of economic and social organization. In one Moslem country university studies of social planning techniques were attacked as a secular threat to the divine dispensation of human affairs. This resistance to alien ideas erupted dramatically in a strong opposition to organized relief for the victims of widespread flood devastation; a programme which, man-made, was seen as a challenge to the will of Allah for his creatures. There is ample illustration of similar resistance to progressive planning in Christian communities.

The particular economic structure of a country may provide another barrier to the acceptance and diffusion of new knowledge. To take one of the most obvious examples: where an agricultural system is based on a system of large landlord estates, the peasants achieving little more than a subsistence level of living, for whom are new ideas important or relevant? In other circumstances, where the land, fragmented through the operation of certain inheritance laws is not economically viable, the contribution of modern science and techniques to agricultural improvement seem just as meaningless. Some recent writers claim that, under these conditions of agricultural malaise, there is little point in talking about 'land reform'. Only a substantial political and social revolution can provide for either a renovation of the agricultural system or the opportunities for applying modern scientific and technical knowledge to the immediate requirements of the country. Whether reform or revolution is the remedy for a particular society, there is little doubt that in many countries of the world at the present time the prevailing economic structure mocks the attempts to introduce fresh ways of thinking and working.

The constant tensions of political leadership in developing countries make understandable, if not always tolerable, the restrictions on individual initiative. In a private conversation, one African political leader stated the position very simply, 'In the earlier tribal groups from which our nation emerged, there could be no opposition to the Chief. Or if there was, it was punishable by death or social expulsion. You cannot expect the leaders of such a new country as this to tolerate quickly the rivalry of other political groups'. Even outside the immediate political arena, deviant opinions about current or prospective activities of the government may be seen as a threat to both the personal power of the leadership and the stability of the nation. Governments vary in the extent to which they possess either the power or the will to suppress such discordant views. But either by direct repressive measures or by giving no encouragement to dissentient opinion, the political authority may maintain a social atmosphere in which novel ideas and innovative practices find no room to flourish. The consequences for national development can be disastrous.

It would be a misrepresentation of current affairs to imply that progress in all developing countries is stifled by the various exigencies mentioned above. To the contrary, some such countries have shown remarkable capacity for assimilating new ideas and for forging novel measures to give substance to new ideas within the educational field. Students in some developing countries have access to a range of knowledge, and participate in educational techniques, that are as yet largely unknown to students of many affluent societies. The syllabus of many a professional training programme in an African, Asian or Latin American country contains a crystallization of modern ideas and practices from many parts of the world; this comprehensive fusion of knowledge and techniques is not always available to the student of an 'advanced' country where traditional academic requirements often limit the scope of a student's experience.

True, these educational measures are often accelerated to excess and there may be cause for disquiet while visiting, in an impoverished country, as the writer once did, a higher educational establishment whose students are top-headed with radio antennae, observing one another through one-way vision screens, and communicating with their teachers by closed television circuits. However, the desire and the will is there to experiment. What is a graver cause for concern is the situation where the vested interests, the fears and sense of insecurity of political, economic or religious élites make suspect not only dissent but even the wish to experiment.

The concept and the use of knowledge in any society sets the boundaries for educational development but many other factors determine the direction and volume of educational achievement. Without any implication that the list is exhaustive, there are ten issues of major importance for educational strategy in developing countries.

Literacy

What steps can be taken to reduce or eliminate the high incidence of illiteracy in many countries? A United Nations Report reveals that at the middle of the twentieth century there were believed to be about seven hundred million adult illiterates, representing 44% of the total world population, of 15 years and over. Half the countries of the world registered 50% illiterate in their adult population. While in the last decade the proportion of illiterates in the world population has decreased, their numbers increase by about 30 million every year. The successful promotion of a development plan depends on the quality of human resources available as much as it does on the possession of material capital. Where a high proportion of these human resources are not only untrained in the specialized skills essential to development purposes but are wholly illiterate as well, planning objectives may be in serious jeopardy.

The problem is not merely one of finding adequate means to develop literacy in an impoverished country. More critical is the dilemma facing governments at present as to what part of an educational budget should be spent on literacy campaigns against the demands of formal educational expansion. This dilemma is heightened by the present lack of knowledge about the most effective measures for increasing literacy in developing countries. Certain examples there are of countries overtaking their illiteracy problem—Russia, Cuba, the Philippines, Southern Italy,

Sardinia, and currently China are amongst these—but some of the most populous developing countries continue to carry large-scale illiteracy as a major economic and social handicap. The governments of these countries are required to make crucial decisions as to how the success of their development programmes can better be served; through massive attacks on the persistent problem of illiteracy, or by promoting the growth of primary, secondary and tertiary educational facilities and, as far as the latter is concerned, particularly higher technical training provisions. The educational budget of a developing country will seldom permit any significant investment in both these exercises.

This either/or situation in the face of large-scale illiteracy is shown plainly in the problems of budget allocation and of the dispersion of scarce qualified personnel for numerous educational tasks. But within these limitations, vigorous attempts are being made, through many social innovations and the use of modern technical devices, to shorten the period and extend the scope of basic education for the illiterate. Community development programmes provide an opportunity for imparting rudimentary education to those without it; formal educational programmes can be designed to carry, without appreciable extra costs, provisions for certain kinds of adult education; courses in training for elementary skills can have an important cumulative effect; the use of radio, television and other technical devices may offer the means to spread adult educational facilities over a size of audience, in a span of time, unattainable only a few years ago. Much possible accomplishment in this field has yet to be thoroughly tested. Some results to date suggest that increased experiment with such social and technical devices may go far in reducing the incidence of illiteracy in many countries.

Two important questions remain paramount with governments confronted with large scale illiteracy. First, do the examples of Russia and Cuba suggest that the only effective answer is a concerted effort to achieve universal literacy? Does a programme aimed at partial literacy accentuate the divisions between the privileged and the under-privileged with negative consequences for the health and potential progress of the society? Secondly, can there be sufficient incentive for illiterate people to acquire skill in reading and writing unless that accomplishment can be given direct expression in work and leisure pursuits that carry important significance for them? In some parts of the world, there is no clear evidence that these two questions have been given the attention they deserve.

Types and levels of education

In 1960, twenty-three countries in Africa, and twelve in Asia, showed a primary school enrolment ratio of less than 40% of that school age population. In the same year, secondary school enrolments of the fifteen to nineteen years age group showed a ratio of less than 10% in thirty African countries and of less than 25% in sixteen Asian countries. The figures did reveal a consistent improvement in all school enrolment ratios over the decade 1950-60. During the decade the most rapid acceleration was of the numbers enrolling for higher education: this was as true for industrialized as for developing countries.

In the context of national development objectives what types and levels of education are required most urgently? On the one hand this involves decisions about the proportion of investment in primary, secondary and higher education; on the other, decisions about the extension of traditional educational programmes and the expenditure on newer forms of technical training appropriate to the purposes of economic and social development. In some countries is found a persisting emphasis on traditional subjects with only marginal value for twentieth-century development. There is often a lack of conviction about the importance of technical education, an attitude which in no small degree is related to the history of the country concerned. Many an African student is more familiar with the Lakeland poets than with the history or present circumstances of his own country.

In determining what shall be spent on primary, secondary or higher education, a government of a developing country may believe that its immediate interests are served by providing a sizeable group in the society with elementary schooling as a sufficient preparation for the more rudimentary tasks of national development. A government elsewhere may see the shortage in secondary school facilities as its most serious educational problem. Yet another government may be convinced that the expansion of higher education, particularly through new and specialized disciplines, offers the surest aid to rapid development. Wherever a government places its major emphasis in educational development, the consequences of its decisions provide new problems for the society.

One consequence will be found in the rising expectations of those being educated. This becomes a 'problem' if the society is unable to provide acceptable opportunities for either employment or further education. Many parents of primary school children may not accept as readily as a government would wish, the limitation of their children's future to the more mundane forms of employment. Most secondary school pupils will be educated just enough to realize that advancement to the top positions will be denied them if they do not acquire yet higher educational qualifications. University students may be confronted, as indeed they are in many countries today, with job opportunities that seem to them not commensurate with their status as a highly educated minority of the community. In developing countries, this is one important factor in the rash of protest marches, riots, 'sit-downs', and other types of boycott whereby students express their anxieties about an unpromising future.

In general, the emergence in any country of an educated group in numbers and variety not known previously, will bring changes in the conception of economic and social need, altering radically earlier ideas of what the society required and should aim at through its planning programme. At each level of education, the pressures generated by social dissatisfaction are inescapable issues for the planner. Yet sometimes they have been surprisingly neglected.

Manpower needs

The nature of educational programming is vitally affected by the anticipation of future manpower needs. A United Nations Report (U.N., 1963), referring to the experience of a number of countries with manpower surveys, asserts the results to have shown that, 'manpower planning and general educational planning need to be developed in close harmony, within the total national development programming effort'. Manpower surveys are essential as a basis for projecting future educational and other social requirements, but with two important provisos:

(*a*) In a developing country it is no easy matter to obtain accurate information about existing circumstances or to reach beyond inspired guess work in any proposals for future social and economic action. To attain even approximate accuracy, surveys require direction by highly skilled personnel and rest on reliable responses from people who understand the nature of the inquiry being made of them. Even in developed countries, which can draw on the accumulated experience of over half a century of social research, social investigation continues to be hampered by the scarcity of suitably qualified professional workers and by ignorance in the community of what purposes social inquiry is intended to fulfil. This is not an argument for inaction when confronted with the complex conditions of under-developed countries, nor a suggestion that these conditions are immeasurable. Perhaps what we need to retain is more caution than has been our wont about the relevance of sophisticated economic and social measurement techniques in developing countries and the significance of the findings that emerge from them.

(*b*) Decisions about the use of manpower are seldom made on a 'rational' basis. Governments have varying political aims, individuals have strong personal feelings about what they want to do and want to be. Either of these influences can play havoc with projected plans for manpower use. How far will a government subordinate certain political aims to a blue print plan for the future dispersal of manpower? To what extent can the government of a developing country direct its citizens to the style and quantity of work considered necessary for effective national development?

A further dimension of this question is the process of change, often both rapid and radical, that cannot be foreseen by planners and which can distort the original conception of what is needed. A dramatic example of this type of problem is given in the January, 1967 issue of the British Journal, *Management Today*.

> The famous example is, of course, the Edsel motor car brought out by the Ford Motor Company in 1956. No industrial product before or since was ever more thoroughly researched. All the 'data' anybody could possibly ask for were collected. But while this was going on, the American automobile market began to change. Customers who had for forty years bought according to income began to buy according to taste. The market shifted from being segmented by income groups into taste segmentation. The figures did not show this. Figures can only show what has already happened. They can only show the 'average', the preponderant. Above all, one can only obtain figures for what one measures. . . . If the tremendous amount of inside information the computer produces makes management neglect to look for itself on an outside which it contemptuously finds

'messy', 'imprecise', and 'unreliable', then management will end up where the Edsel did—on the scrap heap.

The manpower survey expert will claim that all these considerations are well weighed in estimating what exists and what is needed in the future. All that is in question here is the extent to which these considerations are properly understood by everyone of any significance who participates in, and uses the results of, manpower surveys. The implications are crucial for the changing design of educational programmes in any country.

Educational content and methods

In so many countries of the world where a capacity for innovation and the transformation of established institutions are prerequisites for social advancement, both the content and the pedagogical methods of educational programmes are barriers to change. Class-room subjects on each educational level are frequently out-dated and irrelevant to even the country's immediate requirements. It is not uncommon to find class-rooms and academic departments where neither the syllabus nor the text books convey any of the important knowledge acquired by man in the last few decades. Even when the library shelves of a school or department are bulging with up-to-date literature provided by technical assistance programmes, this may represent more their own physical demonstration of modernity than any serious attempt to apply advanced knowledge to the practical issues that confront their society.

Both teaching and learning techniques are often preoccupied with the assimilation and regurgitation of copious and unrelated detail. A final year student may have three major aims: i. The attainment of a 40% pass mark (35% to 37% if 'grace' marks are awarded). ii. The acquisition of exact lecture notes, text book precis, and examination prophecies based on a detailed study of past examination papers. iii. A painstaking committing to memory of all the written material acquired. Only the heroic few may emerge with an intellectual readiness for inventive and integrative thinking. These conditions can also be found in some affluent societies where for a considerable proportion of the population, education has been largely an exercise in repetitive learning, contributing little to the development of any powers of deliberative thought. G. B. Shaw's jibe—that his education was seriously interrupted by his school days—is more than just a Shavian quip, even in the latter part of the twentieth century.

For the developing countries, archaic patterns of education represent an overwhelming threat to their hopes of progress, perhaps even to their prospects of survival. Their need is desperate for planners, entrepreneurs, professional specialists, technologists, skilled technicians—a whole array of leadership for the tasks of economic and social planning. Educational systems which encourage the memorizing of traditional knowledge, which see the teacher/pupil relationship as that of dispenser and receptacle, which afford only secondary status to the preparation in technical skills: these systems are the ones that must be overthrown if a society is to acquire the educational leadership it needs for national development.

Teachers of students from developing countries attending institutes of higher education abroad know the effect these narrow educational procedures may have on the students' attitudes and responses to an unfamiliar academic environment. Difficulties arise at so many points: in understanding a teacher/student relationship so different from their own; in responding to the purposes of the tutorial system; in knowing how to exercise the right to criticize and challenge the teacher; in preparing written material that is more than a compendium of other people's writings; in the discernment of what books are for and how they are to be used; in appreciating the ultimate purpose of a period of study or a course of training. The learning problem all this represents is only partly a question of unfamiliar teaching methods. Often the student flatly rejects both the objectives and the style of a study programme so contrary to his earlier academic experience.

The precise measures that might be taken to deal with the stultifying educational systems of many developing countries are beyond the scope of this present examination. The United Nations and other international agencies, bilateral technical assistance programmes, the educational reforms initiated by individual governments, are giving urgent attention to the requirements of educational change in developing countries. With varying degrees of success these efforts are assisting such countries to increase and redirect their educational resources more purposefully to the objectives of national development.

The educated and the illiterate

A major influence on educational planning in some countries is the attitude of leaders of many kinds towards the uneducated majority. This attitude is often an unconscious acceptance of the 'natural' superiority of the enlightened to the ignorant, superstitious, and tradition-bound mass. Whether or not they know their Plato, such leaders subscribe to some of the less defensible requirements of his proposed Republic. In many places there is strong conviction that by virtue of their original social placement, people are born to command or serve. The history of Europe and, to a greater extent than is often supposed, of the North American Continent, offers ample evidence of a widespread belief in the disparate destiny of two distinct groups of people within the same society.

In the desperate circumstances of some developing countries, where 90% of the population may be illiterate, what has been called the Mandarin syndrome leaves people in authority with little conviction about the value of education for the majority of their countrymen. This in itself will not prevent the spread of educational opportunity—the popular demand for increased educational facilities is too vigorous to withstand—but it may well retard the rate of educational expansion.

Disillusion of the educated

In developing countries, those responsible for educational planning sometimes, but by no means always, give priority to programmes that can best serve the purposes of national development. If not always directly utilitarian in character, such education may yet be designed to produce people appropriately equipped for the tasks of a changing society. At the same time, this may not be the main interest of many who seek the highest educational attainments. For them, education is possibly a symbol, a symbol of hope, of emancipation from the cycle of resignation and despair that afflicts each generation of their families. Two forces at play, national educational objectives and certain individual attitudes to education, are not necessarily incompatible. They may prove to be so for a variety of reasons. Inappropriate educational methodology and the lack of opportunity for the highly educated are two of the most consistent causes of disillusionment with education itself. There are many reasons, political and economic, for the events so often described in our newspapers: students' rebellions, the closure of higher educational institutions, the burning of books, attacks on educational leaders. One reason that should never be overlooked is the high hope turned sour when what at first seemed a miracle of opportunity ends in the old familiar impasse, at a different social and educational level but with little more hope of escape.

Great contrasts exist. In Africa, countries such as Zambia and Malawi may not have been able to number more than a few dozen graduates among their indigenous population at the time of their independence—a critical deficiency for the challenge of national development. In Asia, the more populous countries particularly have been teeming for decades with B.A.s (and failed B.A.s), Ll.B.s and other kinds of licence holders for whom the economy had little to offer but twilight occupations in the courts and the civil service. An urgent task for these governments is the reorientation to modern planning objectives of a sizeable proportion of the educated élite; an élite whose inappropriate earlier studies, and the inconsequential nature of their subsequent employment, have left thousands of them both cynical in attitude and unprepared for the responsibilities of the educated in a changing society.

Types of education required

Most governments are aware that the effectiveness of any one educational programme must depend on the successful implementation of other educational facilities. National planning, if it is to promote the co-ordinated development of a country's resources, must be able to rely on the availability of qualified personnel in a variety of professional and technical disciplines. Such requirements seem to impose impossible demands on the slender resources of many countries, and on the ingenuity of their leaders. The nature of this problem can be illustrated by a brief reference to some of the types of education that seem indispensable to a country's hopes of economic and social expansion.

Education for agricultural development. To a person acquiring his first knowledge of the circumstances of developing countries, there is often something very puzzling in the attitude of governments towards the rural sector of their economies. In a high proportion of low income countries, agriculture is the major production and the majority of the population is engaged in rural occupations. Yet frequently agricultural requirements are neglected while elaborate attention is given to expansion of manufacturing industries and commercial enterprises. Sometimes, among national leaders, this neglect of rural resources seems very close to a lack of interest in what happens to the agricultural economy. This is not true everywhere but when it does exist there are discoverable reasons for it which have been mentioned earlier in this writing. A stimulating discussion of peasant attitudes as they impinge on prospects for agricultural change is presented in Bailey's paper, *The Peasant View of the Bad Life* (Bailey, 1966).

Both the causes of, and possible remedies for, the depressed state of agriculture in many countries are too wide and too deep to be settled by specialized educational provisions. But education for agricultural change remains vital. Where a government is seriously concerned about the need to transform the structure of the rural economy and to revitalize agricultural methods, attention must be given to basic studies and specialized training programmes that will provide on the one hand the agricultural scientists and agricultural economists, and on the other the agricultural extension workers, who are indispensible to any effective programme for agricultural development. No government efforts for the training of agricultural specialists will achieve much without a basic programme of agricultural education for farmers, actual or prospective; along with a schools' syllabus that provides such agricultural knowledge as is relevant for each level of education. Speaking particularly of Latin America, Balogh (1965), states the opinion,

> The problem . . . is not to produce geniuses capable of extending the frontiers of knowledge and devoting to that purpose scarce resources; it is rather to have an educated system capable of inculcating people's minds with the simple knowledge of agriculture and biology as of 1910! You could then double, treble and quadruple agricultural output.

Education for industrial development. In many developing countries, plans for the expansion of industry must include the preparation of people for a whole range of new functions: technological direction, management, foreman supervision, skilled work practices, unskilled industrial activity. Commonly, the traditional educational system has contained little that is relevant to the responsibilities of high level posts in industry. Lower level jobs have to be manned largely by people migrating from rural areas. In both cases governments have little experience or educational resources on which to build an industrial work group. Social attitudes about the status value of certain occupations heighten the problem. In one country, an I.L.O. training consultant, assigned to introduce training programmes for foremen in industry, has found great difficulty in securing applicants for courses, although the salary expectation was higher than that of many white collar occupations where the demand for posts was clamorous. He found that men would not take work that they considered beneath them even for high wages.

In training people for industry in developing countries, governments inevitably are confronted with the task of recovering the losses in their educational systems; of transferring rural people from the cyclical rhythm of agricultural occupations to the year-long repetitiveness of a factory work bench; of persuading people at all levels of industry that their work has positive social consequence as well as providing economic rewards. In most cases, the attraction to industry is in itself no great problem. The promise of regular wages and money in larger quantities than men have known before is enough. This is only the first step; the success of industrial growth will depend on the quality of the educational programmes and training opportunities provided for a wide range of industrial and commercial occupations. A United Nations Report (U.N., 1954; see also U.N., 1958), draws attention to the crucial role of management training for the development of industry:

> Training for management is the most controversial of all phases of training; so far its problems have found the fewest satisfactory solutions. Successful management

demands more than innate organizing ability and occupational skill. Modern industrial processes require an intelligent understanding of scientific discovery; modern commercial organization demands a knowledge of economics, finance and accounting; and the scale of modern operations imposes an entirely new approach to personnel management. There are no easy ways of meeting these requirements, which call for general education as well as technical knowledge. Success at the top level of management may depend to a large degree on the selection of the right individuals to intermediate posts, where they will secure the training and experience necessary to undertake the highest responsibilities a few years later.

Training in administration. Along with the emphasis on management training, increasing attention is being given to the vital contribution to national development of all types of administration—in the public service, in private and nationalized industries, in the organization of professional services. Until recently, most developing countries were hampered by Civil Service systems that were created in, and served the purposes of, now outmoded political and economic situations. Such archaic remnants of an old order persist in some countries bedevilling all the attempts to translate new ideas into effective practice. Governments almost everywhere are creating new types of public enterprises, government or semi-government institutions that require specifically qualified personnel to ensure their success. In low income countries, the development of private industry has been limited partly by the absence of entrepreneurs but often just as seriously by the dearth of people skilled in the exercise of management.

The nature of these administrative inadequacies, and what might be done about them, has been widely recognized. A great spurt of effort to provide appropriate training facilities for the future administrators and managers of developing countries has brought into existence institutes of public administration, administrative staff colleges, business management schools, university studies and special courses in business and public administration, in-service and short term training programmes within public services and private industries. This is one form of specialized higher education to which most countries are now heavily committed.

Adult education. In certain developed countries, there is ample evidence of the contribution made by adult education programmes to a great number of people denied earlier opportunities to continue their elementary schooling. Sometimes this contribution is made through a widening of cultural horizons; at other times it provides the first steps in education for a career. In some developing countries there may be tens of millions of people who have received no schooling of any kind, who are illiterate, and for whom the type of adult education familiar elsewhere can have little significance. Yet illiterate majorities constitute the human capital with which so many countries must determine their future.

In recent decades, the educational efforts of many governments and of some international organizations, chiefly UNESCO, have been partly directed to establishing methods of combating the limited contribution to national development of uneducated and unskilled people. There have been some achievements and many failures so far in the attempts to recover the wastage of potential but uneducated talent. As mentioned earlier, literacy campaigns have made progress in some cases, failed abysmally in others. Something of the dimension of this problem can be understood from a UNESCO Report on Literacy Training (UNESCO, 1967). In the 1950's, in thirty-two countries with a total of 314 million illiterates, only six countries, numbering 26 million illiterates in all, had achieved over 10% enrolment of illiterate people in courses designed for their needs. Community development programmes hold the promise of eliciting people's interest, and exploiting their potentialities, in the establishment of community services. The programmes in themselves are important educational ventures. Imaginative industrial companies are providing simple forms of skilled training for those who cannot read or write.

The pace of progress in most low income countries will often depend on their ingenuity in harnessing to the goals of development the unrealized talent of a large proportion of their population.

The education of women. In nineteenth and early twentieth century Europe, the suffragettes who handcuffed themselves to railings and demonstrated in many another dramatic form, often lived to witness at least the partial success of their early crusade. The final battle has not yet been won as the present economic and social structure of their societies can easily demonstrate. In most developing countries, the first shots have been fired for women's emancipation, but in few of them has progress been rapid. Unequal laws, religious and social taboos, discrimatory educational programmes, restricted public opportunities, all limit the freedom of women to realize their personal and social capacities. In 1960, there were still twelve countries where the percentage of girls in total enrolment in primary schools was less than 30%; twenty countries with a similar enrolment percentage of girls in secondary schools; twenty-five countries with this same percentage of women in higher education (U.N., 1963). This represents a serious deficiency in the resources that might otherwise be available within a developing country. In many countries, as of now, one of the most significant changes in educational planning would be a schools and higher education programme that assumed its common purpose for males and females. The fuller participation of women in the work of a society will depend on other factors than this, but lacking equal educational opportunities with men, women are initially handicapped to combat the many other sanctions placed on their right to engage in all the affairs of the country.

Education for science and technology. The consideration of what contribution modern advances in science and technology may make to the needs of developing countries bristles with difficult and complicated questions. From the wide range of scientific and technical knowledge accumulated in the experience of modern societies, who is to decide what is relevant for the development purposes of other countries? What criteria can be used to reach such decisions? And if we can determine who makes the decisions, and by what criteria, how can such decisions be translated within the cultural and economic circumstances of low income countries? These, and many other crucial questions on the transfer of science and technology are dealt with in a series of Reports issuing from the United Nations Conference on the Application of Science and Technology for the Benefit of Less Developed Areas, which began in Geneva, February 1963 (*World of Opportunity*, 1963).

If one intention is to interest scientists and technicians in the contribution they might make to other societies, can this be effective when what developing countries may need most is knowledge and techniques of a somewhat pedestrian kind? If scientists and technologists discover the greatest challenge in exploring the frontiers of knowledge, how can they be attracted to work situations where they may be separated from direct association with the most advanced developments in their professional field; where also the work in which they are involved may do little to increase their own knowledge or to enhance their professional careers? How many scientists and technologists of its own does a country need? How many can it afford? The answers rest on some clarification of the first questions asked above about the nature of the knowledge needed in developing countries and the means to translate it within the circumstances of a particular society. The ultimate judgments about these national requirements will determine, to a large extent, the type and quality of the curricula at every educational level.

The formal education programme. In deciding what proportion of their educational investment is to be apportioned between the expansion of primary, secondary and tertiary education, governments must assess their educational requirements in the context of a national plan programme. This seems obvious but in fact educational priority decisions are constantly taken with only minimal regard for long term planning objectives. In poor countries, educational advances are slowly won, largely due to scarce resources, but often also because decisions of wide ranging implication are dictated by pressures from parochial interests. Where a high degree of detachment does exist in assessing educational priorities, the process of decision is tortuous enough. When political interests displace more objective assessments of educational need, there may be little hope of attaining an integrated educational programme.

Education for limited qualifications

Pertinent to priority decisions in formal educational planning is the familiar argument that developing countries must accept partially trained workers to undertake tasks that in other countries would be entrusted only to highly qualified people. The argument insists that in the critical situation of many countries workers must be trained quickly where resources are too small to prepare a sufficient number of fully competent personnel; and in any case much of the work to be done can be carried out effectively by people with limited training. This argument is met with stiff resistance from many governments. Along with the professional or technical reasons advanced to oppose it goes a powerful element of national pride. Are developing countries expected to rub along with half baked personnel? At a recent international conference a quite irreconcilable conflict arose between Western European delegates pressing for limited educational aims in developing countries and representatives from those countries who flatly rejected any such attempts at compromise. The deadlock at the end of the conference was due largely to the sensitive pride of some and the obtuseness of others unable to recognize the roots of the resistance to what seemed sensible plans for countries with scarce resources.

In educational programming, as in most other sectors of planning, there is no simple answer as to how many fully trained personnel you need, or what numbers of partially qualified people you can use effectively. If you invest heavily in the second category, what is the risk of repeating the experience of some countries, where workers with only rudimentary training have not been able to fulfil the tasks required of them, partly because they have insufficient skill for the jobs they hold, partly because there are too few people of higher competence to supervise them? Yet it is inconceivable that most low income countries can quickly enough acquire the resources to train the highly skilled personnel they need in such large numbers.

What is beginning to emerge in some countries, often through training plans initiated with the assistance of the agencies of the United Nations and other international organizations, is the establishment of a variety of training programmes which have no exact counterpart in more modern societies, and which seek to prepare workers for carefully defined functions within certain professional disciplines. One example from the field of social welfare is the part-time course that prepares public officials for a wider concept of their responsibilities than is implied in traditional administrative practices. The course is not designed to train voluntary social workers or to produce professional social workers; its intention is to equip government officers for work the volunteer is not empowered to perform and for which there are too few professional social workers to fulfil. In other disciplines—medicine, education, law particularly—courses exist to heighten the skills of workers with only rudimentary training or to qualify new recruits with restricted education for responsibilities formerly given only to those who have completed a full professional education.

These new types of trainees are not conceived of as partially qualified doctors, teachers, engineers, lawyers, but as professional aides for whom a precise role has been planned, and whose training is designed to allow them to perform competently within the limits of that function. An essential accompaniment to this type of training is the preparation of qualified professional personnel for the careful supervision of this new kind of worker. These less pretentious training ventures may provide the greatest possible number of competent workers for the development of professional and technical services in impoverished countries.

Teacher training

What country, anywhere in the world, considers that it possesses an ample supply of teachers, in the quantity and of the variety that it needs? But for many low-income countries, the shortage of teachers may prevent millions of children acquiring any kind of education at all. Against all the other claims on available finances, and no matter what priority is given to educational development, the government of a developing country can afford to train annually just so many teachers, and offer them just so much salary. It has the further problem of retaining the teacher once he has been trained and appointed. In the flux of events generated by development programmes, the teacher may find attractive opportunities elsewhere, more lucrative and with better career prospects. One of the dilemmas for educational expansion in developing countries is that the very opportunities you offer to prospective teachers may suggest to them not only an escape from former insignificant occupations but an eventual route to more enticing jobs. In some countries the situation has been worsened by the practice of governments in plundering the potential teacher group to obtain recruits for other professional occupations.

The outlook is not unmitigated gloom. Governments

everywhere are growing increasingly aware of the importance of human capital throughout the whole range of development planning, aware that it matters enormously for how long and in what way children and young people are educated, aware that the teacher carries one of the most vital responsibilities within the society. This was not always so; one heartening sign in many countries is the changing conviction about the kind and style of education a society must establish if it is to possess any hope of fulfilling its planning objectives.

There is one further consideration relevant to the role of teachers in developing countries. Frequent criticism is made of what is considered to be wasteful expenditure on sophisticated modern equipment in countries where a large percentage of children are illiterate, and where teachers are in desperately short supply. True, such equipment may often be inappropriate for the educational needs of impoverished communities. At other times it may be an invaluable aid in supplementing the work of teachers unable to cope with the enormous demands made of them. Teacher training courses are giving more and more attention to the use that can be made of a wide range of technical aids, some of them very simple in design and execution, which can extend the function of the teacher far beyond the face to face relationship that normally would limit his area of influence. The use of such teaching aids is part of the growing preoccupation with educational methodology as a means to take up the slack where governments are obliged, initially at least, to plan for quantitative results in child education with an alarmingly small supply of teachers. An amusing footnote to this subject was the experience of an English adult education lecturer in Manchester who was demonstrating to a class of overseas students the use of simple teaching materials in developing countries. After a long search, he had managed to locate a pliable plastic blackboard which, if need be, could be unrolled on a tree trunk for teaching purposes. On the day he gave this class-room demonstration, he began a series of extra-mural evening classes in a local Town Hall where no blackboard could be found to illustrate his lectures. For several months his 'bush' equipment, tacked to the back of a door, provided the only visual aid for his classes. Shortly after this experience, he visited a teaching institution in the heart of Africa where instructional aids included closed television circuits, overhead projectors, sound booths for tape recording, illuminated map screens—and revolving blackboards!

The administration of educational policy

In many developing countries the educational administrator is invested with responsibilities that make him almost indistinguishable from the policy makers. There is not always the demarcation of political and administrative functions that exist elsewhere. The administrator may stand between two spheres of influence, each potentially harmful to the future of education: on the one hand, that of the educators themselves who can not always be trusted to set their own house in order; on the other the popular clamour for a type of education that will provide the quickest and most lucrative results. Just because the future of education is so wide open, the administrators' decisions may be the first steps towards a definition of educational policy. This is an awesome responsibility. The training of public administrators, or if so decided, that of a special group of educational administrators, becomes all the more crucial for the outcome of educational planning.

It may be asking for extra-human gifts to expect any government to plot an educational course that will embrace most of the educational requirements mentioned above without at the same time falling foul of the many pitfalls that await the imaginative innovator. Education is a powerful stimulant towards the social change that is a prerequisite and an accompaniment to development. But people will either resist change or may want something from it that does not accord with any official design for educational progress. Education can also provide the diversity of knowledge and the acquirement of skills that offers the individual a role of dignity and satisfying work achievement in the community. Because, potentially, it provides individuals with more equal opportunities, more preparedness for job mobility and greater capacities for using their talents, education is a powerful aid to economic development, ultimately producing a panoply of ideas and skills essential to the establishment of a modernized society. This is a commendable conception of the purposes and possible achievements of education. Sometimes, in some places, and to some degree, these objectives are attainable. Almost everywhere, cumbersome institutions and the perversity of men keep such attainments constantly in hazard. This in itself is no adequate justification for sitting on one's hands. In educational planning, as in all planning, there is as little room for the case-hardened cynic as there is for the self-deluding zealots. Politics, corruption, negativeness, institutionalized injustices, are men and women living together in society. Out of this must be fashioned the education of future generations.

3
Health

Whatever the magnitude of human diseases in many parts of the world today, it is justifiable to begin this examination of health conditions on an optimistic note. Within most developing countries over the last two decades there has been a consistent improvement in the health of their peoples. The latest Report of the World Health Organization (WHO, 1967), shows that the annual general death rate is more favourable, and marked progressive tendencies have been shown in the infant mortality rates, in the expectation of life at birth, in deaths between one and four years, in the number of deaths over fifty years proportionate to all deaths. Considerable success has attended the attack on the highly communicable and the parasitic diseases. Some epidemic diseases have now been eradicated in certain world areas; in other places they have become more consistently controllable or more easily dealt with when outbreaks occur. Both immunological protection and environmental safeguards are limiting the effects of many diseases which often ravaged large populations. As the effects of vaccination, of drugs, of insecticides, take hold, and as measures increase to improve the condition of water, food, sanitation, personal and public hygiene and general living conditions, people are living longer, with less fear of a disease-racked existence.

With all this, there remain three major anxieties for the governments and peoples of many countries. First, the progress referred to above is not universal, either in the number of countries that have benefited from preventive or remedial measures taken, or in the number of diseases that have been combated successfully by modern medical and social planning. Some countries have had only partial success with the eradication of diseases overtaken elsewhere. Certain diseases—tuberculosis is an outstanding example—persist almost everywhere, and in some countries may remain an intractable problem until radical economic and social changes make possible a significant reduction of the affliction.

In our attempts to understand and treat some of these major human diseases we are confronted with the difficulty of determining precisely the effect of specific health measures on the improvement shown in the general health of the population. Many non-medical factors that contribute to personal health—education, housing, employment, even a sense of hope—are easy to enumerate, difficult to measure as contributory elements in improved health conditions. Yet such factors are essential concomitants of health planning. In this context more refined measurement techniques are being sought to assist countries with urgent social priority decisions.

Secondly, a critical shortage of doctors, nurses, hospitals and clinics limit the important results achieved by the breakthrough of the modern medical and scientific attack on human sickness. The 1963 United Nations Compendium of Social Statistics indicates the critical position of some countries which show a ratio of doctors to inhabitants of one to thirty or forty thousand; and a ratio of hospital beds of one to two thousand or more inhabitants.

Thirdly, much of the chronic debility that afflicts a large part of the world population is grounded in persistent economic deprivation and unquestioned traditional habits. To remove either of these major impediments to improved health is a long task for any government, whatever its ideology. Many modern medical practices can achieve only what the limits of an environment allow them. Some diseases—malaria, yaws, smallpox, typhus, yellow fever, leprosy, bilharzia, the virus infections, venereal afflictions —can be treated dramatically through chemotherapy and related mass devices. In most of these diseases, personal living conditions are a significant factor; in some others, tuberculosis and traucoma are obvious examples, the nature of the intimate environment is crucial in the onset and treatment of the ailment. Here, preventive and remedial public health services must play a vital role. Flies, polluted water, inadequate drainage, primitive sanitation, careless food preparation and hazardous eating habits spring from ignorance of hygiene and spread the kinds of infection that ultimately bring death or permanent physical impairment to millions of people.

From this lack of accord between modern medical achievements and negative environments that cannot sufficiently exploit them, arises another dilemma for some governments. Vaccination, drugs, insecticides, large scale drainage, have made possible the eradication or further control of many of the epidemic diseases. As a result, fewer children are stillborn or dying in infancy, adults are living longer. While these consequences of new medical measures provide greater potential manpower for national development, government planning can seldom meet, fast enough, the requirements of so many extra minds and bodies. Man's initiative in one area of applied knowledge has occasioned acute distress where economic and social programmes cannot keep pace with medical achievements. Can a government then refuse to exploit all the potentialities of modern medical science that may be available because it cannot contain the results? If such a refusal is politically inexpedient, how does a government grapple with the consequences of the benefits that medical science provides? The obvious long term answer is in comprehensive economic and social development that will bring within the range of most people the opportunity for continuous and adequately remunerative employment related to the appropriate knowledge and skills that people must acquire for the modernization of a society. This takes time, effort, and a certain amount of luck. For the present, it is difficult to deny the existence of some persistent problems which have been occasioned by the very success of planning.

The medical references so far in this chapter have taken no account of those human illnesses which popularly are considered to be the afflictions of affluent societies, e.g. the degenerative diseases (the cardio-vascular, the cancers, etc.) and mental illness. Present health statistics are not adequate enough to help us understand what the similarity or contrast might be between the incidence of such diseases in affluent and in developing countries. In the latter, the nature of mental illness that exists, the means for diagnosing and treating it, as well as the numbers afflicted by it, are often clouded in obscurity. Within a specific culture, who knows exactly what can be described as mental illness? One of the most significant attempts to grapple with this largely undefined phenomenon is that by a Nigerian psychiatrist, Dr. Lambo, whose highly original work on the etiology and possible treatment of West African personality disorders has led to the establishment of a Department of Psychological Medicine in the University of Ibadan. From such indigenous sources may come more reliable knowledge about the nature of mental illness in developing countries.

One general question begs attention. If increasing information about health conditions in developing countries indicates a low incidence of certain diseases prominent in wealthier societies, are low income countries to expect a rise in the rate of these diseases as their prosperity grows? Will they too reap the results of obesity, sedentary habits, smog-laden cities, the anxieties of the professional rat-race? Who can expect a government faced with crises of famine and possible economic bankruptcy to worry itself about the woes that may come to the fat and the wealthy? But for some countries it may be later than they think.

This last question appears to take on an air of absurdity when linked to the facts of nutrition in many countries. At present, we have all too little knowledge of the degree of under-nourishment among peoples of developing countries. The Food and Agricultural Organization, Third World Survey, 1963, estimated that 20% of the total population of developing countries suffered from under-nutrition, simply having not enough to eat. Perhaps as much as 60% of these populations suffer from malnutrition—an inadequately balanced diet. Reckoning the minimum calorie intake for health needs as between 2,300 and 2,600 per head, several countries in Asia, Africa, and Latin America were well below this level as late as 1965 (FAO, 1966).

In general, we do not know enough about the nutritional requirements of populations within the tropical zones. What is considered essential as a nutritional minimum in temperate climates may be no satisfactory guide to the needs of people elsewhere. An urgent task for governments of developing countries, possibly in collaboration with international organizations, is an investigation of the nutrients required to provide basic health conditions among their citizens. A valuable start has been made through the work of a Protein Advisory Group, sponsored by UNICEF, FAO and WHO, which advises these agencies, and through them the national governments, on current knowledge about protein deficiencies and the simplest measures that may be taken to combat them. Medical research programmes of the WHO are examining the factors associated with nutritional anaemia, the significance of certain diet deficiencies in the onset of blindness, and the relationship between nutrition and infection.

Where so much ignorance exists about dietary needs, increased prosperity may mean that people simply eat greater quantities of unsuitable food. Rapid population increase distracts attention still further from the consideration of vitamin and protein values. Where the race is desperate to keep food production abreast of the increased numbers of mouths to feed, a qualitative improvement in diet is not easily foreseeable.

New sources of nourishment now being explored—from the sea, from the cotton seed, groundnut and fish flours, from the byproducts of industrial waste—may provide foods which are both rich in nutriment and more cheaply produced. Two recent developments are of potential promise. British Petroleum are producing food virtually from nothing by growing protein on oil waste. In a plant they propose to begin in Marseilles in 1968, they expect to turn out annually about sixteen thousand tons of concentrate. Ranks, Hovis, McDougall, Britain's largest bakery combine, are experimenting with the use of flour waste, producing a mould that converts some of the carbohydrates into protein in the course of the growing process. One cwt. of flour waste produces about thirty pounds of pure protein, plus essential fats and mineral salts. The Company hopes to have a commercial pilot plant by mid-1969 and a plant giving three hundred tons of protein a week by 1970. The B.P. process needs oil but no foodstuffs; the Ranks process may serve better that half the world, without oil, which is vegetarian and protein starved because meat is too costly (*Sunday Times*, 1967).

Within the next decade or so, our knowledge of dietary deficiencies in developing countries will grow, as will our understanding of the measures that might be taken to overcome them. This will be only part of the answer. A nation's eating habits are not easily changed, whether they are day trippers from Dover roaming the streets of French coastal towns in search of bangers and mash, or rural dwellers of Asia and Africa whose diet is part of the fabric of social and family history, of birth, death and marriage, of religious sanctions, of the cycles of the seasons, of the inexorable toll taken by generations of poverty and tedium. It will be a long haul to prepare the peoples of developing countries for the acceptance of unfamiliar dietary elements in their daily food. Surveys undertaken by FAO, WHO and UNICEF indicate how little attention is given to diet requirements in the curricula of schools and universities, even in medical schools and in public health training courses. Perhaps the most effective starting point for an appraisal, and ultimately the fulfilment, of a society's nutritional needs, is the establishment of a national food policy, a measure yet to be taken in many countries.

What then, are the most important considerations for health programming in developing countries? No great feat of the imagination is required to state what some of these must be. It is something else again to speak with conviction about the means for realizing them. At least, as an act of clarification, we can look at fourteen requirements for sound health planning. If some of them appear to be statements of the obvious, it becomes all the more a matter of concern that the obvious has been so frequently overlooked.

Health planning

Measures to attain the highest level of health possible for a whole population must be seen as a vital element in development planning, determining both the volume and the quality of national achievement.

Health administration

Training programmes must be established to prepare more specialized personnel for general health administration and for hospital administration, the latter training focused on new concepts of the function of a hospital within a community.

Co-ordination of social services

More attention must be given to the essential relationship between health and other public (or private) services. Lamentable deficiencies in social welfare programmes have often arisen where this relationship has been misunderstood or sometimes not even recognized. It is not uncommon, for example, to find such mutually dependent services as public health and education conducted by separate government departments which show little interest in the co-ordination of their respective programmes.

Health education

In many countries health education must be raised above the well meaning but often farcical level of public media propaganda. Where, as in one large Asian city at present, only contaminated water, dung from diseased cattle and devitalized food scrapings protect millions of hovel dwellers from almost immediate death, the conditions for effective health education defeat the imagination. In other, more promising places, health education requires a blend of rigorous community training and subtle personal appeal far beyond the methods of exhortation so commonly used.

Medical auxiliaries

In developing countries attention must be given not only to the training of more doctors and to their retention in the country (from one Asian country recently, statistics revealed a greater number of their doctors working abroad than remained in their own services) but to increased training for medical auxiliaries. However unpalatable this proposal may be to the medical profession, auxiliaries, under competent medical supervision, could reach and offer limited but beneficial treatment to large sections of the population otherwise denied assistance. One of the most significant recent publications on health in developing countries states, 'any task, which has to be repeated many times, even though it is comparatively intricate, should, if possible, be taught to an auxiliary' (King, 1966).

Rural health services

Implied in the last consideration are the urgent medical

requirements of rural peoples. One of the grave imbalances in developing countries is the concentration of professional services in the cities and towns. It is only part of a much wider issue to point to the need for a greater regionalization of health services. This is already a trend in some countries and must be accelerated if rural areas are to survive as viable units of a national economy.

Community organization for health

The response to community health services, as well as the range of their benefits, may well depend on the participation of local people in the organization of health programmes. This means more than just the localization of medical facilities; it implies the involvement of prospective patients in measures designed for the treatment of personal and social health deficiencies. Some countries have already made important achievements in their organization of community responsibilities for medical care. Among others, the Egyptian social centres are important illustrations of what local participation in health programmes can achieve. In poor societies desperately short of medical personnel and hospital facilities, community organization for health needs can be a powerful resource.

Rural urban migration

The influx of rural peoples to the cities and towns is a phenomenon known throughout the world. In low income countries the strain that such movement imposes on urban areas already deficient in most public amenities represents a serious health hazard. Few such countries have prepared for the consequences of this migration or dealt effectively with its results. This is not surprising. Money, materials and expertise are all inadequate for the increased social demands of swollen city populations. In all this the threat to human well-being is more than what is shown in squalid living conditions and over-taxed community services. There is the additional problem that we know little about the precise effects on human health, both physical and mental, of the social dislocation of rural peoples migrating to urban areas. The extent of this ignorance challenges the attention of health planners everywhere.

Nutrition

Reference has already been made to the diet deficiencies causing serious malnutrition among many peoples, and to some of the measures being taken, or considered, for the correction of inadequate food intake. Here, at least three major issues demand serious inquiry. First, wherever malnutrition is widespread, are people under-nourished because they are too poor to buy healthful food, because they are ignorant of what food properties are required for their nutritional needs, or because they are resisting the changes in food habits necessary to a better diet? In many cases, each of these factors may be exerting some influence on the continuation of a deficient diet. It is all too easy to attribute cultural origins to attitudes and practices that are largely a result of poverty. Secondly, surveys in developing countries—one of the most recent among Mexican Indians—have shown that the 'natural' diet of a group may be as nutritionally beneficial as the planned food habits of a vitamin-conscious society. There is good reason to believe that in many countries a fresh examination of existing or potential local foodstuffs, and their treatment for purposes of human consumption, could relieve the present state of malnutrition without recourse to the costly importation of additional food. Thirdly, those who work most directly with the problems of human nutrition are conscious that the relationship between food and health involves more than the amount of vitamin and protein intake. The study of nutrition entails a study of the whole man in his total environment. This is not to underestimate the dramatic physical improvements that have followed the specific changes in a people's diet; but for any individual the enjoyment of robust and continuous health demands a condition of physical and emotional well-being not usually attained even in affluent societies. Within this broad context lies the proper understanding of the relationship of diet to human health.

The curative and the preventive in health planning

In countries where the volume of human need far outweighs any present or any anticipated resources to meet it, health planning may be confused by one particular dilemma: namely, the relative emphasis to be given to the curative and preventive in national health programmes. If, as some planners have seen, there has to be a choice between these two measures, the professional rationale for any such choice may be completely discounted in the political repercussions to the decision. The nature of the choice for health planning has been stated quite simply by many medical men in developing countries. There are not at present, nor will there be in the foreseeable future, sufficient doctors, nurses, dispensers, and other health personnel to treat effectively more than a minute proportion of the widespread sickness, chronic or more rapidly fatal, in the population. The concentration of medical facilities on the treatment of this small percentage of sufferers is a misdirection of a crucial planning resource to ameliorative purposes that can have no lasting effect on the improvement of the nation's health. A considerable part of the existing medical resources must be directed to determining the appropriate preventive measures—legislative, administrative, medical, social—that could provide a framework for progressive health planning.

If this is the exact nature of the choice to be made, that is, between limited resources being dissipated on non-progressive treatment services, or those same resources being directed to devising supportive measures for long term health planning, then the outcome in any country might be determined by the nature of the answers to two questions. Are there a sufficient number of highly qualified medical personnel with both the imagination and the toughness of mind to support the direction of a large part of the country's medical resources to the planning of long term preventive health programmes? Does the government hold the kind of authority to allow political decisions that are not related to the immediate interests of its present citizens?

Current experiments in some countries are searching for possible measures to combine the curative and preventive aspects of medical care. One innovation has been the establishment of rural health centres designed to promote more effective public health programmes and to provide also medical services for the family. In some places these rural units are designed as social centres, giving a wide connotation to the definition of health, including provisions for adult education, citizens' advisory services, community councils, and a number of other facilities that encourage the citizen to participate directly in the planning of services for his own community and to take some responsibility for its most urgent needs. In emphasizing the crucial role of health centres in developing countries, the following axiom is presented following an authoritative health symposium in Makerere, Uganda: 'Some form of medical care should be provided to all the people all the time. This is based on the value judgement that it is more desirable for moral, political and other reasons to provide some form of medical care to many people rather than to provide a complete service to only a few' (King, 1966).

Hospital services

In developing countries, a new conception of the function of the hospital is imperative. That at present it is overcrowded, under-staffed and dangerously insanitary is an understandable, if not defensible, symptom of underdevelopment. The hospital service is often seriously deficient in two other respects. It may lack any close association with the work of the private medical practitioner or with the public health services of the community. It may also be limited to a few areas of urban concentration, its facilities beyond the reach of the majority of the country's population. Such a hospital service provides little opportunity for either curative or preventive medical services on any effective scale, let alone their integration within a comprehensive health programme. Radical thinking in the replanning and distribution of hospital services is one of the most urgent measures for the health programmes of developing countries.

The general medical practitioner

Whatever benefits community health planning and a reorganized hospital service may bring, the general medical practitioner represents a keystone in the structure of a national health programme. We are only beginning to give attention to the qualifications and the training required of such a professional person in the critical conditions of low income countries. Is he to be, as a WHO report suggests, 'a new type of general practitioner, better qualified to deal with the problems of preventive and social medicine, mental health and family pathology?' Can such a professional person embody both the curative and preventive approach to medical care? Again, to what extent should his training anticipate the many different functions he may have to fulfil from one part of the country to another?

The answers to these questions are not easy to find. Their implications, and the urgent need to provide answers to them, are stimulating within international organizations and national health associations discussion, research and experiments in comprehensive health planning that may relieve the sufferings of this generation while building the hope of sounder health for the next.

Mental health services

In February 1967 a B.B.C. television play, written by the

head of a hospital psychiatric unit, depicted in a young woman the process of disintegration to a state of acute schizophrenia. Part of the fierce newspaper correspondence that followed was in condemnation of the social and hospital conditions that contributed to this woman's deterioration, but most of the letter writers were rejecting the substance of the play itself. The author was attacked for the emphasis he laid on certain contributive factors in the onset of schizophrenia; some critics would not agree that the condition so dramatically described was schizophrenia at all. The arguments, in support or rejection of the author's thesis, were waged with a great weight of medical knowledge and experience. The layman could be excused for suspending judgment about the psychiatric veracity of a compelling drama. He could also be justified in believing that in a technologically advanced society there is still a high degree of uncertainty about the precise causes of, and available remedies for, different states of emotional illness.

In those vast tracts of land a few degrees above or below the equator, where a great part of the world's inhabitants live, conceptions of the causes and cures of mental illness often resemble those prevalent earlier in Europe (and still to be found there among those who will have no truck with scientific explanations of behavioural abnormalities). Incarnation of the Divine, demonic possession, the casting of spells, pre-natal shock, a malignant birth date—these are only some of the popular explanations of erratic human behaviour. As vivid are some of the favoured cures: mortification of the flesh, scarification by fire, immersion in water and flaying of the skin, traditional incantations, bleeding, ritualistic sacrifices, sacred herbs and potions, the laying-on of hands—and many other means of exorcizing the evil inhabitant. Anthropologists have documented the many varied interpretations of, and panaceas for, mental illness.

For any developing country the problem of mental illnesses, if it is not to continue as a neglected social deficiency, raises two difficult questions. First, how can an impoverished country acquire the insight and the expertise to define and understand the treatment required for mental aberrations whose characteristics may be largely derived from a particular national environment? How much do we know as yet about the relevance to developing countries of the psychiatric experience accumulated over three-quarters of a century in Europe and North America? Secondly, whatever the prospects of determining that which needs to be done, and how, about mental illness, what attention can the government of a developing country give to a disease whose treatment requires the resources of expensively trained personnel, a large ancillary staff, specialized equipment, and a network of domiciliary and outpatient services. Is it economically justifiable or politically feasible to direct more than a very limited amount of development funds to this aspect of social need? The obvious corollary to this last question is doubt as to the effectiveness of any partial measures to deal with a complex human condition.

The response of some governments to the awkward problem of mental illness has certainly not been an attitude of inertia. Despite the daunting requirements of money and specialized personnel, some governments have already established Departments of Psychological Medicine in universities or teaching hospitals. This represents only the beginning of psychiatric treatment services in some countries; in others little or nothing has been attempted. Among a large part of the world population, the understanding and treatment of mental illness remains an urgent task.

Medical research

The foregoing paragraphs should in themselves indicate the need for more medical research about the precise nature of indigenous diseases and the kinds of resources required to prevent or cure them. Some results of modern medical experience are directly relevant to the health needs of developing countries, others are not. The Makerere Symposium (King, 1966), whose published report runs to several hundred pages, begins, 'Proposition one. That medical care in developing countries differs sharply from medical care in industrial ones.'

More extensive research should reveal how many illnesses in developing countries are amenable to treatment by modern medical resources, if and when such resources are available; and how many illnesses may defy accurate diagnosis and any confidence about appropriate treatment. In both affluent and low income countries Schools of Tropical Medicine and Hygiene are providing valuable contributions to our understanding of the climatic, economic and cultural factors associated with the origins and treatment of the insidious illnesses among a great part of the world's population. The work of certain international agencies—WHO, FAO, UNICEF are among the most prominent—is extending this understanding by experiments and demonstrations designed to illustrate the possible remedies for a variety of diseases that hitherto, unchecked, have frequently decimated whole populations. Further medical research is imperative to provide a clearer description of the events that invoke the endemic diseases of some countries and to provide a better knowledge of what can be done by developing countries, within their limited resources, to cut at the roots of malignant growths that threaten most of their populations.

4
Social Welfare

The definition of social welfare

There is a certain vagueness about the meaning to be given to 'social welfare', particularly in relation to developing countries. We can attempt to define the term, although there appears to be no definition that meets with universal agreement. Perhaps the most widely accepted is the United Nations' description (U.N., 1963), of social welfare as a wide range of socially sponsored activities and programmes directed towards community and individual well-being. 'Social Services' are then identified as a more limited specific functional area within this broad grouping. 'Social work' describes the professional activity primarily concerned with social service functions. One could employ several hundred words in either explaining these definitions or in challenging their adequacy. The most serious contention is that they do not describe any distinctive quality or activity essential to the fulfilment of the economic and social objectives of national planning. A current expression of this attitude in one developing country is the insistence of the Secretary for Planning that all the measures directed to development are purposive to social welfare, which has no valid meaning as a specialized activity or a special professional discipline. In this particular country, the statutory and private social welfare agencies, and the Schools for Social Work Training, are engaged in a tense argument with a key government department which barely accepts their right to existence. For one or another reason, in national affairs and at the level of international organization, social welfare as a concept and a practice is widely misunderstood, sometimes rejected, and occasionally accorded no more than a peripheral role in the determination of planning objectives.

What then is the important contribution that social welfare organization and practice may make to both the definition and satisfaction of human need? Among the many possible ways of answering this question, perhaps the use of illustration is the best starting point. For this purpose we may take four categories of people with whom social welfare is commonly concerned: children, delinquents, the disabled, women.

The child

Indisputably, many of the issues that determine the fate of a child in any society are essentially economic: the financial resources of his parents; the health and educational facilities available to him; the later prospects of employment. But, as the present experience of many countries can show, there is no absolute connection between a society's degree of affluence and the state of its children's well-being. Visitors from developing countries who spend any length of time in the wealthier societies are increasingly puzzled by the contradictions they find within them, not least as regards their treatment of children. The prevalence of the battered-baby syndrome is the more dramatic occasion of their concern.

Amid the desperate poverty of some lands, those who plan for a brighter future see in the increase of personal wealth and the improvement of educational and health opportunities a guarantee of greater well-being for the children of the nation. In the wealthier countries, whose citizens enjoy a level of economic sufficiency unobtainable by most of the world's population, there is growing concern, and official action in response to it, about the incidence of child neglect and other forms of cruelty to children. Governments have been obliged to appoint Commissions of Inquiry, introduce special professional training programmes, erect new buildings or enlarge old ones, and outlay large sums of money in an endeavour to understand and treat a serious social problem. Visitors from developing countries are often naïve in their expectations of what wealth will bring. What they see of child problems in an affluent society must lead to a disturbing reappraisal of the possible developments in their own societies. It would be overstating a thesis to pretend that economic issues were irrelevant to an explanation of why an advanced society ill-treats so many of its children. However, the evidence emerging from many enquiries in developed countries suggests that the reasons for the ill-treatment of children are rooted as much in forms of personal and social maladjustment as they are in factors of economic deprivation. There is substantial support for the conviction that the remedies for this ill-treatment of children will be found primarily through the provision of personal counselling and community care services. This is the stuff of social welfare, and any country which underestimates its importance risks, on the one hand the contraction of the potential talent available for nation building, and on the other a growing incidence of unhappiness and sense of frustration among its population.

The delinquent

From the deprivations of childhood experience may emerge the later delinquent, although what the exact equation is here we are still not sure. The blend of interior and external factors that provoke an individual to anti-social behaviour is even now improperly understood, despite the great volume of appropriate research and professional experience in developed countries. Barbara

Wootton has given some important illustrations of the caution with which criminal statistics should be treated (Wootton, 1959). In other lands there is even greater uncertainty about the origins of, and possible remedies for, delinquent behaviour. What has emerged from the wealth of studies and practical experience of criminal activity is a sense of caution in explaining its nature or in suggesting prescriptions for its remedy. It seems evident that in most cases a combination of personal and material factors, difficult to measure with any accuracy, occasion delinquent behaviour; it seems just as probable that any effective rehabilitation of the delinquent, or any action to combat the forces that give a shape to delinquency, must direct primary attention to the significance of this combination of the personal and material associations of criminality. In the broad sense, this is a social welfare task, pooling the contributions of sociological, psychiatric and economic knowledge to determine appropriate treatment of the delinquent and the wider social measures that might reduce the incidence of delinquency. In many developing countries action against crime, other than through the operations of the traditional law enforcement agencies, is not always given a high priority in national planning, although many governments, with the help of the United Nations, have established regional institutes to prosecute research and training in the causes and treatment of delinquency. (See following U.N. publications:

Asia and the Far East Seminar on the Prevention of Crime and the Treatment of Offenders, Rangoon, 25 October-6 November, 1954 (U.N. publication, Sales No.: 55.IV. 14); *Second Asia and the Far East Seminar on the Prevention of Crime and the Treatment of Offenders, Tokyo, 25 November-7 December 1957* (U.N. ST/TAA/SER/C/34); *Latin American Seminar on the Prevention of Crime and the Treatment of Offenders, Rio de Janeiro, 6-19 April 1953* (U.N. publications, Sales No.: 54.IV.3); *Middle East Seminar on the Prevention of Crime and the Treatment of Offenders, Cairo, 5-17 December 1953* (U.N. publications, Sales No.:

54.IV.17); *Second United Nations Seminar for the Arab States on the Prevention of Crime and the Treatment of Offenders, Copenhagen, 23 September-16 October 1959* (U.N. ST/TAO/SER./C/42).) Yet the problem remains of considerable national importance. Crime in the sense of reported offences and registered convictions cannot be separated from pervasive attitudes and activities in the society that, within or without the law, may constitute a serious hindrance to social and economic progress. Delinquency in the legally definable sense is often but a fragment of a wider malaise that is the proper concern of social welfare activity.

The disabled

In developed countries, considerable attention has been given to the rehabilitation of the disabled person. With the conviction that useful employment will maintain his feelings of self respect and his sense of contributing something to his society, special training courses and attendant services have been devised to equip him for a productive work role. Unquestionably the results have been beneficial to great numbers of partially incapacitated people, but those professional helpers who have worked most closely with them know that even a useful job and a regular wage are not always sufficient compensation for a certain loss of identity. Much depends on the character of the person and the nature of his disability. Some may never be reconciled to their loss, others may need specific professional or social support to sustain it. Often this support has been the decisive factor in their ability to adjust themselves to a new job and a different life situation.

The present plight of many low income countries may appear to rule out any serious concentration on the requirements of disabled people. Whether or not attempts are made to train them for useful work, they are often, in numbers alone, a significant group in the society. For economic reasons, in terms of human happiness or suffering, as it affects the self respect of a country, such people can be ignored only at considerable cost. The cost may be reckoned and written off as unavoidable, but one way or the other, the welfare of a society is at stake.

Women

In a recent discussion on the place of women in present day European society, a member of the suffragette movement of the early twentieth century stated that the causes for which women fought today were different from those in the earlier decades. She was not explicit as to what the new causes were but one is made aware of them from the words and decisions of women in our time. There remains a sense of their subordinate economic and social status and of an insufficient use of their potential talents in society at large. One marked feature of modern European society, the increasing number of married women taking salaried employment, rests on one or more of three primary motivations. First, the need to add to the family income. Secondly, the wish to exercise potential or neglected talents. Thirdly, the desire to be able to dress each morning for a claim on one's time outside the house, and its inexorable repetitive demands.

In developing countries, the issues activating European women have implications for only a small group of educated women who have found a new freedom in the life of large cities. For the rest, their role is one of overt subjugation to the male, whatever the influence exerted from the kitchen and the bedroom. In some countries women are isolated from any direct contact with society at large. These conditions represent both a curtailment of human freedom and a loss to the society of unexploited abilities. To fight for equal educational opportunities for women, for their right to enjoy economic and social freedom alongside men, is to fight the centuries old taboos which support present inequalities. Often, social welfare workers, whatever their original anticipations of it, find themselves engaged in the struggle for women's emancipation from the thraldom of ancient traditions.

A reader with only a rough knowledge of social welfare may consider that the paragraphs above belabour some rather obvious points. They do indeed, but in some countries it is by no means evident that these simple facts about the role of social welfare activities have been understood or accepted. In the strategic centres of government planning there is frequently to be found a conception of social welfare as a fringe activity, expendable when other urgent priorities claim the nation's attention, more permissible where economic circumstances are favourable to its expansion. Echoes of this attitude can be heard along the corridors of some international agencies.

The interpretation of social welfare

Those who are concerned with the exposition and development of social welfare policy are grappling with two major obstacles. First, the persisting image of social welfare as a Lady Bountiful activity in whatever sophisticated guise it may now be presented. Secondly, the failure of the exponents of social welfare to justify its philosophy and expediency to the decision makers of national planning programmes. There are indications now that these obstacles, if still of sizable proportion, are shifting under the weight of attack from national and international social welfare movements. The sharpening of their ideas and the accumulation of wider comparative experience are developing in social welfare workers an increasing confidence in the validity of their central role in national planning. Nobody has done more to assist this clarification of social welfare purposes than the social agencies of the United Nations. Certainly, for the outcome of planning programmes in developing countries, the conception of the role of social welfare in national development is of crucial significance.

In low income countries, no matter how mature the understanding of human need and what is required to meet it, social welfare programmes are operating within a national context of financial deficits, a shortage of qualified personnel, inadequate institutional structures. In a few countries where special circumstances prevail (e.g. of size, of homogeneity, of natural resources, of the type of labour forces available) some limited scheme of social security may be feasible. In other countries, where even simple income tax assessment is not workable, nothing of the kind is possible in the foreseeable future. With scarce funds, few people equipped to undertake professional responsibilities, and no organizational framework for the expansion of services, social welfare programming must be inventive and highly flexible. There must be forged a definition of social welfare, and plans for its implementation, that belong to the soil in which it hopes to flourish. The growth of community development programmes; the efforts of social work educators to free themselves from foreign professional ideology and to establish an identifiable form of local training; the formulation of a new design for welfare services among rural people; these are only a few of the measures being taken to establish indigenous patterns of social welfare activity. In some cases these activities may require the use of traditional structures for the transmission of social welfare services; in other cases, a modification or radical alteration of existing institutions. Innovative devices are necessary in societies cramped with the inertia of centuries. To each country will belong an idiosyncratic pattern of social welfare activity.

Here emerges the ambiguous presence of the bilateral or international consultative agency. For so many countries struggling to clarify their design for social welfare, the external agency has been able to provide invaluable support. Unfortunately, not all such assistance has respected the indigenous assets available or known how to relate the experience of a modern society to the circumstances of a developing country. More will be said of this in a later chapter; the issue is too central to leave without even a reference here.

Social welfare priorities

As with planning for education and health facilities, the tortuous question of priorities confronts social welfare programmers. Decisions as to the priority to be given to social welfare within the plan for national development may rest partly on some of the circumstances discussed earlier in this chapter but just as often on a range of fluctuating and unpredictable events. Domestic politics, international alliances, the policies of aid-giving agencies, will play as great a role as any local analysis of the requirements for social welfare.

Within the limits set by national planning decisions, social welfare policy makers must determine what attention should be given to short-term emergency measures, how much to long-range planning of preventive services. What should you do about the crippled, the blind, the hungry, the chronically ill, the delinquent? All the resources at your disposal can hardly make a dent on the problems represented; every penny you spend reduces your chance of providing more radical measures to cut the problems at their roots. Strong political pressure will be exerted on social welfare organizations to provide dramatic relief measures. Public understanding will not easily accept the reasons for investing in long-term planning measures.

This dilemma for social welfare planners can never be resolved in the context of such a debate. The answer must be found within the society itself, through its people and its institutions. There is merit in illustrating here, some of the measures taken to this end in a number of developing countries.

Community effort for social welfare

One of the most significant activities is that of community

development. Called by a variety of names from one country to another, and directed to many different purposes, its major aim is to stimulate people's belief in their capacities for self help. In many parts of the world, community development activity has harnessed the potential abilities of whole communities to tasks of economic and social improvement. The progress of such work has provided new community services, volunteer workers' training courses, child and adult education classes, work opportunities, liaison with government services: at a financial cost fractional to that which any official programme would have entailed. Even by its most ardent advocates, community development is not claimed to be a cure-all for the economic and social ills that beset low-income countries. It does provide an effective demonstration of what people can achieve by community effort even in circumstances of great poverty and lack of public services. On these beginnings can be built more substantial social welfare programmes. The literature of community development, both from national and international sources, is now extensive. For this present discussion, two publications may be noted: The 1963 United Nations Report *Community development and National Development* (Sales No. 64.iv.2); and the *Community Development Journal* (Oxford University Press), a quarterly journal edited in Manchester, England.

A key figure in the community development programme is the voluntary worker. He is required urgently in many social welfare activities other than community development. In some countries, where the extended family system is the traditional base of community life, working without pay for the society at large is not a familiar practice and does not come easily. One important task, and sometimes the most difficult, is to select and train voluntary helpers for service in private welfare organizations, in clinics, in institutions, in villages and small communities. Not for many years to come will many developing countries possess even the rudimentary professional services to make comprehensive welfare programmes effective. In the meantime, assistance to the present skeleton staff of specialists must be provided by either voluntary or partly qualified assistants. Here the importance of inventiveness and flexibility is apparent. There is little room for doctrinaire views on the minimal requirements for professional accreditation.

An important issue associated with the development of community participation in social welfare work is the co-ordination of government responsibility for social planning with the efforts of citizen groups or voluntary welfare organizations. If social welfare is to become a significant element in national planning, governments must accept greater financial and administrative responsibility for its direction than has generally been the case in the past. The temptation in this for political band-waggoners is obvious. A great deal of nonsense has been spoken and perpetrated in the name of 'the people' by both politicians and others who find another route to power and public fame as champions of the deprived citizen. Ludicrous indeed are some of the attempts at political identification with the suffering masses. Only one of numerous such incidents was the carefully planned visit of a governmental minister to an impoverished village. Dressed in the rough spun cloth of local craftsmen and coached in the use of local dialect, he made his entry and departure in a chauffeured Mercedes Benz!

This is not simply a black and white issue. Important achievements have been made by politicians and other do-gooders whose motives for identifying themselves with welfare activities are mixed indeed. The central problem remains as to how the responsibilities of government can be fulfilled adequately while allowing the widest possible opportunity for community initiative. Some countries, through the support of authoritative national and regional social welfare councils, have demonstrated both their preparedness and their ability to establish an effective co-ordination of statutory and voluntary social welfare programmes. In other places, governments have believed, justifiably or not, that the degree of political and social stability within the country could not allow any widespread permissiveness of citizen organization. A third pattern can be seen in the country that has not yet accepted the indispensable role of social welfare in national planning, where welfare activity is left largely to private groups, groups which have not the money, the personnel, or the authority to provide anything more than limited remedial services.

Social wastage

This is one of the most damnable features of low-income countries. Within their shortened circumstances much potential talent and social opportunity is discarded from ignorance, through the inertia imposed by archaic institutions and customs, by an inability to exploit the facilities that exist to promote social development. No better example of this last deficiency could be found than in the unwillingness of government agencies to co-operate in joint ventures where their combined functions have an obvious contribution to make to the welfare of the society. Government servants will frequently admit this shortcoming but rarely their own culpability in it. In one country with a large population crippled by chronic diseases, a Medical Officer of Health saw clearly that a successful public health programme must depend, among other considerations, on an efficiently organized educational campaign. He sought to enlist the co-operation of the Ministry of Education in a joint health and educational venture to provide information about public hygiene. Neither the senior official in the Ministry of Education nor his opposite number in the Ministry of Health was willing to be seen making an overture to the other. No normal machinery existed for such discussions and finally the Medical Officer of Health wrung an agreement from each official that he would be prepared to attend any meeting for the purpose that might be called by a third party. This was done through the initiative of an interested professional worker and a year after the proposal was advanced the first design ever was drawn of a co-operative plan for an education and health programme in public hygiene.

This no doubt is an extreme case. The formulation and implementation of development plans require a close co-ordination of work between government departments if the plans are to work at all. Yet much remains of earlier disinclinations of government ministries to co-operate with one another. The slender resources for social welfare activity are further reduced where government departments are unwilling to share their facilities and combine their purposes in following social welfare objectives. This organizational shortcoming is but one example of the administrative deficiencies that in so many countries lead to the squandering of human talents and other resources vital to the purposes of national development. Political caprice, economic exploitation, antique customs, take further toll of already scarce assets.

Selective social planning

A government confronted with deep-seated social ills but with little money to relieve them may resort to one or more limited forms of social assistance, using as criteria for their choice what has come to be known as a system of selective entitlement to social benefits. This system may identify one group of people with a particular social need, e.g. children who have been deprived of family care. Or it may direct its attention primarily to those whose economic circumstances are desperate even assessed by the prevailing living conditions in the country. For this purpose the operation of a means test is unavoidable, although its effective application is a hazardous procedure in certain countries. A further method of selective entitlement, with an eye on the future as much as the present, is that of contributory social insurance whereby obligatory savings help to protect people against familiar ills—prolonged sickness, disability, loss of a breadwinner, unemployment, etc. The 1963 United Nations Report on the World Social Situation includes a thoughtful analysis of the possibilities of selective entitlement.

However limited and restrictive the earliest provisions of a system of selective entitlement may be, the method does provide the basis for a more inclusive pattern of social benefits as economic wealth increases. Detracting in no way from what has been said of the value to a society of voluntary effort and community self help, the measures required to deal with the major social needs of any country are far beyond the capacities of even the most enthusiastic and enlightened private welfare organizations. Resources of the State, albeit pitifully small to begin with, must be deployed to meet the most obvious threats to a nation's present and future welfare. And if, in determining who shall be helped, this means one kind of discrimination, better so than the paralysis of good intentions nullified by confused loyalties.

The historical context of social welfare planning

Finally, as concerns what social welfare might be in a society and what it might achieve through its citizens, attention must be given to the historical antecedents of present day social planning. In most developing countries, whatever the signs of change discernible now, ancient customs and traditional social structures have provided over the centuries a collective support for the individual, child or adult. The tribal pattern of relationships, the extended family system, initiation, marriage and kinship rites, religious assurances; through these institutions and practices societies tried from their limited resources to meet the needs of their members.

All over the world, societies which for generations have known a largely static existence find it no longer possible to withstand the force of change. Modern forms of transport and communication bring ideas in and take people out; national and cultural isolation is breaking down; new forms of employment in fast growing cities and towns impel individuals into a market economy and away from a family-based subsistence economy; the pace of change is frequently dislocating the traditional relationships of the generations and the sexes. Knowledge of what might be is creating widespread dissatisfaction with the nature of things as they are. These manifestations of change are producing social expectations and social problems which the traditional institutions, in their existing forms, cannot serve effectively. In some instances they may be sufficiently adaptable to adjust themselves to tides of change but they cannot expect to achieve this with either the speed or the resources required to cope with new social demands.

The introduction of modern social welfare programmes often must begin in circumstances where traditional institutions are losing their force but where little else exists to support the development of social services. At this point social welfare provisions are inevitably rudimentary, restricted and lacking the institutional or administrative framework that ultimately must be an essential condition for the effective use of social services.

5
The determinants of social policy

Economic factors

Making full allowances for all that has been said about the contribution of social effort to national development, social planning in any country is largely conditioned by the extent of its economic resources. The wealthier nations, where they have introduced comprehensive social security systems, have been able to do so because their industrial and commercial growth, and their ability to operate both personal and indirect tax assessments, have provided a reliable basis for continuous and expanding social services. Certainly, other factors than their degree of wealth gave impetus to the development of social security in these countries, but without the economic resources to support it, social planning on any national scale would have remained the idealism of the dreamer.

The economic facts are grim for much of the human race. Nearly half of the world population live in countries where the annual income per head of population is £25 or less. People of these countries earn less than 10% of the world's incomes. Conversely, people in the wealthier nations who represent less than 25% of the world population, but earn nearly three-quarters of the world's incomes, show an annual income per head within the range £330–£800. Overall, 85% of the world's population live in developing countries, which embraces most of Africa and Asia, Central and South America, most of Oceania and large areas of the Mediterranean basin; the remaining 15% share about 90% of the world income and gold reserves and nearly 95% of the world's scientific capacity. This minority of nations produce 50% of the world's wheat, 70% of its meat production, and 80% of world protein.

Income per head figures may not be the most accurate indication of a country's wealth, and money statements given in any type of currency must be interpreted variously as applied to one country or another. Still, the above figures do provide some idea of the dimension of the problems of social planning in low income countries, where neither the general economic resources nor the levels of personal income provide a financial basis for comprehensive social security provisions.

What are the prospects for accelerated economic growth in those areas of the world now only a little above a subsistence level of living? Even the experienced economist may be reluctant to offer anything more than a highly qualified answer to this question. Particularly so when it is obvious that a wide range of political, social and international influences may, at any one time, assist or impede the prospects of economic growth. There are, nevertheless, some signs of advance, however imperceptible they may be to the casual eye. In varying degree from country to country, more money is being invested in durable capital projects; improved techniques are being employed to locate and exploit natural resources; successful efforts have been made to improve the flow of energy, transport and communication; more food per head of population is available; income per head of population has risen; greater numbers, and even percentages, of children are attending schools; the ratio of doctors to the number of population has improved; and the last chapter described the progressive measures taken in reducing the incidence of disease. Although the figures must be examined in the light of many qualifications, the rate of growth of the gross domestic product has shown, over the last decade, an annual increase per capita of between 0·5% and 6·0% for a number of developing countries. Among the mass of academic writings and reports of international bilateral agencies associated with economic development in low-income countries, the 1966 O.E.C.D. publication, *Government Organization and Economic Development* is particularly informative about both the intentions and the results of co-operation for economic development between aid-giving agencies and individual governments.

At first sight this is all very encouraging, but the evidence is incomplete without the recognition of two other vital factors. First, world population is growing more rapidly than even the optimum forecasts of the demographers have allowed. From a figure of 1,000 million in 1830, world population had reached 2,000 million by 1930, and over 3,000 million by 1960. Even conservative estimates by demographers, working with international agencies, suggest a population of over six billion by the year 2,000 (Lambe, 1967). Much of the fastest growth is in developing countries, often outstripping their rate of food growth and the rise in national income. Allied to a fall in the general death rate and a rise in the expectation of life span, some developing countries are discovering that all their efforts at economic reconstructions are nullified by the inexorable demands of a swelling population.

Secondly, a much publicised 'widening gap' between the rich and the poor countries represents more than feelings of frustration and envy when other countries are seen to be growing proportionately richer. A more serious threat to developing countries comes from the movement towards greater self-sufficiency within the more affluent nations where technological advances in providing for domestic consumption needs reduces the former degree of dependence on external sources of supply.

A proper economic analysis of the circumstances and requirements of developing countries is beyond the scope of this present writing. The simple point stressed here is the inescapable economic limitations to social welfare achievements in low income countries, however imaginative the planning measures may be.

Political factors

For the last decade, the writer has been associated with public administration training courses for senior government officers from developing countries. In both formal class-room discussions and in private conversations, one issue as much as any other preoccupies the attention of the group: the relationship of the politician and the administrator as it affects the work of government in its broadest sense.

Not only do the forms of political power differ greatly from place to place; the means for determining and implementing government policy also show wide variations. In some countries—Latin America demonstrates many such cases—the political and the administrative function is not clearly distinguishable; this may include regimes where administrative personnel assume and relinquish office with the changes of political fortune. Elsewhere, to whatever extent it is abused in practice, the public administration unit by statute is an independent career service. In any of these situations, what is seen to be the domination of the politician produces constant anxiety among those responsible for the organization of government services.

The politician, whether he is elected to office or assumes it arbitrarily in the name of the people, believes that he is expressing the popular will and that he has a more sensitive finger on the pulse of national feeling than has anyone else. Understandably, if often unjustifiably, he is impatient with the dry caution of those who may try to remind him of some of the realities with which he has to work in a developing country. In relation to social welfare planning, this may occasion a conflict between the hogwash of political demagogy and the efforts of planners and administrators to establish services that are workable within the economic and social limits of an impoverished country.

In one country a startling example of this conflict arose within the relationship of a Minister of Social Welfare and a local university. The Minister, recently appointed to office but with no experience of social welfare activity, called to an interview the Principal of the university and a senior education official. His proposal, more in the nature of an order than a request, was that the university should organize a two-weeks' course for its thousands of students as a preparation for undertaking social welfare activities in the villages of the country during the long summer vacation. The prospect was so appalling to the two men concerned that they risked the political repercussions of their refusal to accede to the Minister's demands. Incensed at this stubbornness the Minister then insisted that on the last day of summer term he be provided with microphones on the campus when he would instruct the student body as to the services required of them among people throughout the summer. At this critical point providence intervened in the shape of an international organization which offered the Minister a six months' Fellowship abroad. By the time he returned, his government had fallen, and he was out of office. International organizations also can move in a mysterious way.

The conflict between political purposes and realistic planning objectives is not usually as overt or as dramatic as the last illustration depicts. Nor is political intervention necessarily a negative force. Frequently, it represents the only hope of breakthrough where opposition or inertia strives to maintain a *status quo*. In any case, planning decisions are largely political decisions. The prospects for social welfare are dependent on politicians, sometimes on one man, the Minister of Social Welfare. A fragile thread to weave a pattern of social welfare for millions of people! It was said of one African economic planner that his early death in a road accident cost his country at least a decade of development. Social welfare can be a cliff-hanging exercise where the moods of politicians and the availability of a tiny number of leaders may signal advance or retreat in social planning.

Cultural factors

To those from outside who advise a country on its social welfare programme and to those inside who have direct responsibility for social planning, there are three possible pitfalls when assessing the weight of cultural factors in the determination of social welfare policy. One, it is all too easy to universalize the social welfare experience of other societies and to dismiss as ignorance, reaction, or vested interest, the resistance to unfamiliar ideas and practices. Two, it is as easily possible to over-estimate the effect of cultural drag and to be so preoccupied with the threat to traditional values as to induce a state of paralysis. Three, there is a constant danger of ascribing to cultural forces what is not rightly attributable to them, as, in an example already given, the disposition to interpret in cultural terms certain human attitudes which have their origins in economic poverty more than anything else.

If some of the progressive social welfare measures described in the last chapter are to be made effective in developing countries, many established ways of thought and traditional practices must be either jettisoned or considerably modified. Stultifying religious orthodoxy, uncritical attachment to ancestral habits, a constrictive view of the nature of man and the world he inhabits, xenophobic attitudes to the new or the 'foreign'—these are the influences that arrest the spread of enlightened social welfare planning and, of course, other aspects of development. Social welfare planning at one and the same time may be seen as threatening to usurp the rightful functions of the family and as an exercise of vainglory, abrogating to itself the power and the wisdom that belongs to the Creator.

This is strong stuff and is not presented here as typical

of either the attitudes or behaviour of people in many different places. But personal beliefs and traditional systems are frequently barriers to social progress as at other times they can provide the opportunities for change.

In each of the three major areas of social need we have examined, education, health and social welfare, time-worn practices will not be lightly abandoned. For centuries untrained midwives have been the only source of help for millions of women at childbirth. In the absence of professional medical aid people of all ages have learned to rely on the medicine man and 'native' cures for all ailments. In community affairs the elders of the group have been both the source of authority and the arbiters of the forms of education essential to the members. The amount and type of work required of any individual was regulated by immediate family needs. With the exception of the matriarchal societies, the economic and social welfare of women was carefully prescribed by dominant male authority. In its various forms the pervasive social grouping was the extended family, where blood ties were the first imperative of social responsibility.

The family

Through all the vicissitudes known by many people in centuries past the extended family system often provided the only assurance of economic survival and social cohesion. Despite its valuable historical role, and the contribution it continues to make in many places, the extended family system may yet be a restrictive influence on social planning. The absolute claims of the family can diminish the stature of the individual and demand of him an economic and emotional allegiance inimical to the contribution he might make to national development. When the first claim on him is the joint interests and expectations of the family group, he may have to forego opportunities for higher education, travel, the kind of employment in which he is particularly interested, the personal choice of a marriage partner, the ultimate decision about the future of his children. For a woman the restrictions are even more decisive. One remembered incident is of a Moslem girl who in defiance of parental prohibitions climbed each morning from the window of a locked bedroom to attend social work training classes, there to seek class-mates' opinions on photographs of young men presented by her parents as possible marriage partners.

Where the extended family system remains deeply embedded in the social structure, there will be an inevitable conflict of loyalties for those who challenge its authority. But many are doing just that, trying to find in a smaller family unit more scope for personal initiative and involvement in the affairs of the society as a whole. Sometimes the conflict for the individual may be lessened where current economic and social influences are modifying the traditional family structure. If this not be the case, for both the individual and the society the ancestral pattern of family life may represent a major obstacle to social progress.

In some societies a paradox exists where a family structure designed for the protection and care of the individual militates against the best interests of the child. Voluntary organizations and government departments concerned with the welfare of children have been confronted with stiff parental opposition, particularly to the implication that the extended family system is not adequate to meet the basic needs of children. Again, because of this kind of social resistance, some social work training institutes have not found it easy to include in their syllabuses teaching on family and child care. To the members of many a traditional family group, the use of professional facilities for children requires a surrendering of the child to impersonal, amoral forces. For parents, there is also the threat to their livelihood where children make an important contribution to family subsistence. The traditional family structure cannot provide the essential health and educational requirements of a child; it can retard the progress he might otherwise make in a world of growing opportunity.

Celebrations

One other cultural factor not always given the attention it deserves is that associated with many forms of personal spending. There is no reliable means for estimating the costs to the individual and the nation in the inescapable obligations of private hospitality or in the expenditure incurred by public celebrations in many developing countries. The custom is widespread that any family members, and they can be numerous indeed, can rely on a relative's generosity to house and feed them during visits made to his locality. As a consequence, it is by no means uncommon for a government official to prefer a post in a remote area to one more lucrative in the capital city. By the frequency of their visits to the capital, his relatives make it too expensive for him to survive where obviously his best professional opportunities lie. Recently, an overseas government official studying in Britain was found plotting a tortuous journey home through the most deserted regions of his country that he might escape the obligation to shower gifts on hosts of relatives to be found along the more obvious return route. Certainly, among family members the provision of hospitality is reciprocal but it can become a crippling burden on those who must succeed. While all this has its farcical element there is a serious implication for social development in a family practice which can impair the individual's contribution as a citizen of a wider community.

The costs to the individual of private and public celebrations are easier to assess. The writer once worked with a young man who, at the time of his marriage, was earning 80 rupees a month (the exchange rate at that time being 16 rupees to the pound sterling), with prospects of only small annual increments in the foreseeable future. The two days of his nuptial celebrations—the continuous feasting, the exchange of gifts, the wedding clothes and other appurtenances—were at a personal cost of 8,000 rupees. Most of this money was borrowed at an extortionate interest rate. For the greater part of his life, a high percentage of his salary would be returned to the money lender. To provide an acceptable dowry his wife's parents bound themselves in similar debt. This is not an extreme or unusual example of marriage arrangements. Thousands of families live perpetually in the shadow of huge debt repayments, with wedding expenses as one of the major causes of their poverty.

Religious festivals, fiestas, seasonal celebrations are frequently conducted at high personal and national cost in countries that cannot adequately feed and educate their young. To be in Rio de Janeiro during Carnival (and what misanthrope would refuse such an opportunity?) is to be aware of the dramatic contrast between the golden excesses of the occasion and the unrelenting poverty that afflicts most of the population. This celebration represents the best-known of many such extravagances in impoverished countries. As with wedding costs, the expense to the individual of the brief fiesta may exhaust his present financial resources and burden him with future debt.

Weddings, festivals, carnivals, private and public celebrations: is he who criticizes the 'wastefulness' of these occasions a sourpuss who believes, mistakenly, that the path from poverty to affluence is the straight line of rational, prudent development planning? Does such a critic fail to understand the temperament and traditional attributes which constitute the genius of a people; that this, among other needs, is what planning has to serve?

In whatever way one is disposed to answer these questions, some factors in the situation are crucial for social planners. The expenses of private celebrations and recurring public festivities leave the individual and the family no margin to contribute to their own social advancement. If the state is to be considered as a major source of social assistance, another issue arises. The total cost of the many traditional activities described above is far more than the direct expenditure involved. For each occasion and often for weeks during any one event, the efforts of perhaps millions of people are diverted from essential economic activity to the creation of a world of rainbows. The officially-sanctioned holidays alone can sometimes represent a serious threat to effective work output. In one country, excluding the weekend break and annual leave, formal holidays provide most workers with an average of three quarters of a day free each week throughout the year.

A society which cherishes particular traditions may place the cost of preserving them high in its list of priorities. The cost may well be the contraction of opportunities for social advancement. But if the final freedom is to allow man to go to the devil the way he chooses, what sanctions will planners justify to curb the extravagances of a traditional society?

Tradition and change

A fundamental problem for a social planner is in understanding the extent to which any particular set of personal convictions and traditional habits may tolerate new ideas and practices. How true is it that an Islamic society, with its touch-stone of Koranic teaching that is practical and explicit, provides an effective impetus for the growth of modern social welfare practices? Does the wide embracing toleration of Buddhism induce inaction in the face of problems that should be met with vigorous attack? What is the future for social welfare achievement in societies who see the individual man as a shadowy figure in the drama of the ages rather than as a person growing to stature within his lifetime? The social anthropologists, among whom Margaret Mead is perhaps the most widely read, have given us valuable insights about the conflict of tradition and change; but we need to know more about the way religious and philosophical convictions condition a society's attitudes to change.

Two facets of our ignorance are of particular importance. First, we cannot properly say how far the questions of the last paragraph refer to stereotypes rather than to any national realities that exist in the world today. Secondly, we have only brief experience as yet in testing the response of traditional societies to modern social welfare practices or in assessing the relevance of these practices to the social requirements of developing countries.

In trying to forge new instruments of social policy, we are thus confronted with a number of questions which seldom permit a satisfactory answer. In a particular society, what degree and style of change will the existing cultural context allow? Of what nature is either the resistance to change or the forces that may assist it? When is there justification for challenging head-on the retroactive elements in a static society? In determining the requirements for welfare planning, how relevant is the social achievement of any other country? Are we sure enough of the means by which achievement elsewhere can be adapted to indigenous circumstances and needs? To what extent is it possible to distinguish cultural factors from the political, economic and personal issues that determine the shape of a society?

If any man, or group of men, possessed the wisdom to answer these questions, the golden years for many millions of people might not be far away. As it is, we have to learn from our mistakes as much as from our achievements the permissible degree of social development in countries where the claims of the past strongly condition what the future may hold for their impoverished populations.

National defence

Geography and size have produced in Costa Rica a freak among nations; a country without an army. Elsewhere defence planning takes an enormous toll of national resources. There is perhaps little need to reiterate here the familiar arguments about guns or butter. Enough to say that, oil sheikhdoms apart, the developing countries for purposes of military expenditure are forced to restrict their social development. This problem confronts most governments and perhaps little can be done about it by any one country until there is more general agreement about the reduction of arms throughout the world.

There are, however, two interesting characteristics of the military establishment in developing countries. First, in those nations where the armed forces have taken over political command, military leadership has often demonstrated a strong sense of social justice and a capacity for planning constructive social welfare measures. This is certainly true in a country like Pakistan, whatever criticisms there may be of the political measures taken by President Ayub's administration. Secondly, in countries where, paradoxically, a critical shortage of specialized personnel does not provide a wide variety of career prospects, the defence forces offer three attractions: a regular job; opportunity for specialized education and a sense of identity with a purposive group. We need not be surprised that, to use S. E. Finer's (Finer, 1962) ascription, 'the man on horseback' should so often be both ready and able to assume the direction of national affairs.

In the light of events in a number of countries, how much of their military expenditure can be reckoned as gain or loss to national development defies any exact analysis. There is no reliable yardstick for measuring the strength of arms required by any nation to ensure, in the current international situation, a secure basis for social planning. Military spending for war or the threat of war plays havoc with the prospects for social welfare development. But national security and a sense of national pride are social realities as significant as the bread-and-butter issues of welfare planning. When, after the disastrous rout of the Jordan army in the Israel-Arab conflict of 1967, King Hussein was asked about the greatest future problem facing his country, he replied that it was the loss of dignity occasioned by defeat. His conviction was that before any fruitful development was possible in Jordan, she must find her soul again. For so many peoples the prospects for social development are inseparable from their sense of destiny. In this context is to be adjudged the impact of defence costs on social welfare planning.

International aid

The growth in the volume of aid to developing countries has been one of the most significant international events since the Second World War. The total amount of such assistance given during the last two decades is not easy to assess but some figures from the early sixties indicate the extent of both bilateral and multilateral aid. In the years 1962 and 1963 the multilateral agencies dispersed an annual average sum of 821 million dollars to developing countries. In the same period the annual average total of bilateral aid from four countries alone—The United States, United Kingdom, France and Germany—amounted to 5,041 million dollars. The dimensions of foreign aid and the political ramifications for the donor and the recipient have been given attention in a number of recent publications; one of the most concise yet comprehensive accounts is that given in *Effective Aid*, published by the Overseas Development Institute (London, 1967), based on the proceedings of an international conference. In the current pattern of international technical assistance there is both promise and threat to social planning in developing countries.

Aid in a variety of forms—capital grants, loans, food, equipment, consultative services, study fellowships, travel allowances,—has for many developing countries become an indispensable, irreversible element in their national development. Increasingly, the provision of aid is being related to the implementation of development plans, often as a condition of any assistance given.

To what extent there has been effective use of aid eludes

precise measurement. The results of aid may only be seen after a considerable lapse of time; there is the further difficulty of estimating at what date a measurement should be taken of aid benefits. These are not insuperable problems. Most technical assistance agencies, international and bilateral, are establishing better measurement criteria, often building into their aid machinery the means for assessing the effectiveness of their programmes. The United States Agency for International Development has recently completed a world-wide survey of the consequences of the aid given to foreign trainees studying in the United States on American Government scholarships. The results of the survey, now published in a number of reports (A.I.D., 1966), will be amplified year by year in a continuing assessment of this form of aid.

The interests of the donor

In looking at the purposes, provisions and effectiveness of international aid as one of the important determinants of social policy, certain issues are paramount. Should aid donors be considered as legitimately involved in the determination of social policy? What are the risks of interference in decisions that rightly belong to, and indeed may only endure if made by, the people of the country concerned? How far can you reconcile the anxieties of a donor about what seems to him misspent aid with the demands of the recipient for some independence in deciding one's own destiny? From the innumerable occasions that this issue has arisen two examples may serve to illustrate the nature of this conflict between the giver and the aided.

In one developing country of some fifty million people, a group of international social welfare advisers found themselves in protracted argument with local officials about measures to be taken for the relief of poverty, unemployment and physical disability. The advisers, looking at the problem in the light of national planning objectives, were anxious to see established legislative provisions for a limited range of social benefits, extensive work programmes, rehabilitation training, and community-initiated services that could supplement government planning. The local officials, while ready to accept the wisdom of these proposals as long term objectives, would not agree that they had any relevance for the immediate future. They proposed the establishment throughout the country of institutions to provide on the one hand ameliorative services for the disabled and on the other, a rigorous work routine for street beggars and others described broadly as 'idle' members of the society. To the protests of the consultative group that this was nineteenth-century thinking about social need and its fulfilment, the officials' rejoinder was an insistence that neither their plight nor their remedies for it could be compared with what prevailed a century ago in Europe or America. Further, they insisted that they must be allowed to make their own mistakes in the process of learning what was appropriate to their situation.

No early resolution was found to this conflict of opinion. As so often happens, dramatic political changes in the country took the issue out of this arena of debate. But while it remained as a controversy between advisers and officials, fundamental questions were raised for both donor and recipient about the role and the rights of each in the process of giving aid.

Recently, in the capital city of a large African country, a number of its planning officials argued in a seminar with international consultants the appropriate means for defining and implementing planning objectives. The officials, most of them youngish men, had all profited from training abroad, had read all the right books on development planning, and were convinced of their current ability to advise the country about planning priorities and the means to translate them into effective action. In the seminar discussions there was a curious reversal of the roles that are often supposed to exist when local officials meet international experts. On this occasion, the international group was making a strong plea for a sounding of public opinion about planning priorities, a plea rejected by the local members. In their opinion, a population largely illiterate, widely scattered and engaged in menial occupations, could hardly be the source of any inspiration for planning ideas. As one African member asked, 'Are you suggesting that we issue a questionnaire to the nomads?' The officials were convinced that as a group of highly trained specialists in an educationally backward nation, they constituted an élite that could be the only hope of enlightened planning.

In this African country the argument remains squarely where it began; local officials and international advisers continue to debate this critical issue of planning, a debate which inevitably raises questions as to how far you can go in assisting someone whose aims or methods you cannot approve, and on the other side, how much you can tolerate of the 'interference' of those you have asked to advise you, and who, if they are worth having at all, will bring with them extensive experience and forceful ideas. We must examine a little further the ambiguous role of the international consultant and the ofttimes ambivalent attitudes to him among the persons he is sent to advise.

The international consultant

The consultant is a person with a triple allegiance: to his international agency, to the government he is advising, and to the country which has nurtured his ideas and experience. Until recently, (and continuing as a significant element in consultative services), the international adviser has been a person whose educational accomplishments, social conditioning and professional or technical expertise have stemmed from an industrialized, technologically advanced and highly urbanized society. How far is such a person capable of examining his own clutter of social and professional preconceptions in determining what part of his experience may be relevant to the needs of a very different type of society? The short answer is that he can never achieve this high degree of perception about himself and his mission. It is possible, however, to discern one of three major responses in the international adviser to the challenge of an unfamiliar environment and unfamiliar tasks.

First, the consultant may adopt the somewhat doctrinaire view that the country he is advising must develop attitudes and methods that in affluent societies have been the mainspring of their progress. He may often be right about this, and the argument may be more concerned with how this is to be done rather than whether it should be done. If, however, the consultant insists that both aims and methods of social development should be in close accord with the experience of affluent societies, he is likely to provoke widespread resistance to his ideas or to encourage impoverished countries towards costly mistakes. In many countries the culturally conditioned attitudes of international consultants have often imposed unrealistic planning aims, inappropriate planning structures, over-elaborate administrative organization, extravagant and often irrelevant training ventures.

Another response by the international consultant to an unfamiliar work environment may be one of confusion or even despair. Technical assistance assignments can be tough and rough affairs. Removed from the professional resources and many other facilities he has learned to take for granted in his own country, the consultant must display both a high degree of resilience and a lasting sense of humour if he is to cope with the political, cultural and economic realities that seem to mock at his intentions. Not all professionally experienced people are equipped with these personal qualities. One consultant, a man of outstanding reputation in his professional discipline, laboured vainly for three years in the foothills of the Himalayas seeking to advise a group of mountain dwellers on the organization of social welfare programmes. Finally, an urgent message reached his agency that he was gravely ill and arrangements were made to fly him out by a hospital plane service. In layman's language his illness was described as nervous exhaustion and those who talked with him at this time were convinced that his breakdown owed as much to a sense of personal frustration as to any other factor. The international agency, anxious to understand exactly what had happened, sent another member of its staff to talk with the leaders of the mountain communities. He found among them a deep concern about the consultant's misfortune. They had come to hold the deepest liking and respect for him and his labours among them, and expressed the hope that when he recovered, he might quickly return to work with them.

The descent to confusion or disillusionment is not always so dramatic for a consultant, but the seeds of it are always there for anyone who takes his terms of reference seriously. Many a consultant sees his assignment through with a kind of cynical stoicism; some take the next banana boat out; others fashion the first draft of their next book. The experience of such consultants can hardly be the substance of aid agencies' annual reports; they are nevertheless a significant element in international technical assistance.

A third type of response to strange circumstances is that of the consultant who can jettison enough of his professional conditioning to examine objectively the economic realities, the political climate, and the cultural heritage within which his work must be done. In any advice he is offering to local people, the consultant will be impelled towards the innovative, the tentative, the experimental, in search of a programme design that will accurately reflect the known requirements of the society and the particular genius of its people. One of the ironies of international work is that on this issue some of the stiffest battles for the consultant can be with his local counterparts who may believe their surest road to progress is the route taken by the developed countries. The consultant's reluctance to accept such panaceas for local ills may engender confusion or hostility among his indigenous colleagues.

The distinctions among international consultants suggested above are rarely so clear-cut. There is found among them, however, a tendency to react to their assigned roles in one of the three ways described. The consequences for social planning can be profound.

The interests of the recipient

And what of the other partner in the technical assistance scheme—the recipient? Does he see the purposes and use of aid in the same light as the consultant or the consultative agency? The repeated demand of developing countries for aid without strings is unrealistic in the present world situation but it conveys an attitude towards technical assistance arrangements that cannot be ignored. How far is it possible to reconcile the interests of the donor with the freedom of the recipient to determine his own objectives and even the measures taken to fulfil them? For the recipient, the answer to this question rests on his clear-sightedness about the nature of social need and what international aid can do to assist it. The answer is also partly to be found in the courage that can resist the intellectual moonshine that masquerades as expertise in some technical assistance programmes. The courage to call down a bluff depends to a large extent on a sense of self-confidence. It is at this point, with their limited professional experience, that local people are vulnerable in the presence of the foreign 'expert'. In one planning consultation between government officials and international consultants, dealing with the requirements of fifty million people in an Asian country, one official alone opposed the consultants' carefully prepared plan for social development. He challenged it as a 'rational' statistically based set of proposals that had taken no proper account of either the political or the cultural climate in which it was expected to flourish. Subsequent events proved him right but at the time he had little more than intuitive 'reasons' for his rejection of the plan proposals. He risked his future career in speaking out against the arguments of the experts and the silence of his native colleagues.

Assuredly, technical assistance relationships are not all of this character. Local people can be obscurantist to the extreme; consultants can often be more perceptive about what is politically and culturally permissible than indigenous people bound by personal commitment to traditional values and practices. The local official remains a powerful force to be reckoned with, and even at his most tiresome is saying and representing something about the immediate situation that cannot be ignored by those who wish their plans to move from the blueprint to the life of the village and the town.

The international technical assistance agencies with their increasing provisions of training and wider professional opportunities for local people are helping them to a greater knowledge and sense of confidence about their own affairs. As this process continues, the man in the seersucker suit and the button-down collar will become less the oracle, more the adviser, who works with local people knowledgeable and imaginative in their grasp of social planning requirements. This has already happened in some countries; in others, time, internal dissension, the luck of the draw, are some present decisive factors in the speed of their progress towards greater self-awareness.

6
The Instruments of social policy

Legislation

The drafting of laws that can provide an effective sanction for social action is a complicated and exacting task. A blend of high legal skill and considerable working experience is essential to the efficiency of the parliamentary draughtsman. In Britain somewhere between fifty and one hundred Bills may be presented annually for the Royal Assent. By amendment or re-drafting they have to meet the challenge of opposition parties of both Houses, alternative proposals from Government members, representations of pressure groups, and even after-thoughts from the original sponsors. Keeping pace with the necessary revisions demands of the draughtsman thoroughness and the ability to work fast.

To prepare a Bill for its passage through a legislative assembly involves more than legal expertise; it requires an exact understanding of parliamentary procedures; of the roles that members of the assembly play in shaping new legislation; of the functioning of the party system where it exists; of the powers of a second chamber; of the authority of the Prime Minister/President and the official Cabinet; of the electoral system which supports politicians in office; of the pressure groups that can influence the success or failure of specific legislation; of the relationship between the Assembly, the Executive and the Public Service; of the authority of the Courts *vis-à-vis* the political assembly and the executive.

He might wish to deny it, but it seems obvious that the legislative draughtsman must possess strong political acumen. Any Dickensian image of him poring over the minutiae of legal niceties in a slightly musty law enclave hardly fits the facts of existence in the turbulent world of present-day politics. Legislation is for political purposes, to meet social objectives in a society with conflicting aims. Laws that are designed without regard to these realities are in peril. The draughtsman, among others, can never afford to forget this.

In the colonial past of most developing countries, expatriates were mainly responsible for the preparation of new legislation and the clarification of its relationship to customary law. In some places the education of native people for future legislative tasks was given serious attention; in other places, the colonial authority provided little opportunity for the development of local expertise. The Congo remains a sombre reminder of the consequences of such neglect. J. M. Lee's recent publication (Lee, 1967) makes some pertinent points about the changing roles and attitudes of colonial administrators at various stages of British imperial power.

Whether or not colonial regimes encouraged the development of indigenous legal ability, the legislative tasks for developing countries are formidable. Often against a background of fluctuating political fortunes, inefficient administration (inefficient largely because it is inappropriate), grave economic poverty, lack of skilled human resources, the draughtsman is asked to frame legislation that is legally defensible and politically and socially acceptable. All this in countries where religious laws may remain as imperatives and where some traditional practices are as binding as any legal sanctions. In those Moslem societies where Islamic law decrees the clear differentiation of male and female roles in respect of family rights and obligations, the care of children, and participation in public affairs, what kind of social legislation could provide effectively for progressive family welfare measures? In a country where the capacity of the extended family system to care for all its members is a matter of cultural pride, what are the implications for legislation on child care, old age, disability, delinquency?

For a wide range of need in developing countries social legislation involves more than the provision of a legal framework for the extension of social benefits and social services; it also carries a challenge to traditional attitudes and established practices in the conduct of family and community affairs. In developing countries, as elsewhere, the effectiveness of new social legislation will depend to an important degree on the capacity that politicians, parliamentary draughtsmen and administrators show to combine professional expertise and social perceptiveness in their designs for social development. Such qualities among legislators may not always readily be found in Europe, the North American continent and in Australasia, where continuing social blunders, legal mistakes and administrative inefficiencies are committed by legislative groups possessing a rich store of knowledge and professional expertise and further able to draw on long experience of legislative debate and parliamentary procedure. For new nations this has to serve as a reminder of the skill, patience and the social insight required to construct a legislative programme realistically attuned to both the needs and the necessary changes in a particular society. A recent publication (Burns, 1966) has explored the extent to which British legislative and administrative experience might assist those who are at the early stages of their Parliamentary experience.

Administration

In most developing countries, whatever official encouragement is given to voluntary enterprise, the determination of social policy is largely the responsibility of government. The organization of administrative services to implement policy decisions is a crucial element in social planning. Almost everywhere, in their expansion of administrative training facilities, governments are giving recognition to the key role of administration in social development.

Just as successful law-making rests on other factors than precise legal skill, effective public administration requires more than the ability to formulate and apply administrative regulations. The syllabuses of administrative training units around the world are more and more revealing this conviction. The public administrator, especially at the senior level, is an adviser to his minister and sometimes, inescapably, a not inconsiderable voice in the determination of policy. He is also, at every level, a public official, frequently the only continuous representation of government known to the citizen. This dual responsibility makes him a significant figure in the planning and execution of social welfare programmes. The practical issues arising from this administrative function deserve some consideration here.

Frequently, the administrator has received a higher formal education than the politician to whom he is responsible, has enjoyed professional training for the tasks he has to fulfil, and has benefited from specialized studies abroad. He is required to relate this knowledge and experience to the political motivation of his minister. He may decide to acquiesce in all the minister's proposals, seeing himself simply as the executor of political decisions. This can be carried to ludicrous extremes, as on one occasion when an Asian minister of social welfare, anxious to forestall popular criticism of favoured treatment to any one section of the country, planned the establishment of his social welfare centres at an exact mileage distance from each other. This plan located one of the centres in the middle of a vast desert. No public servant challenged the proposal and at the eleventh hour it was left to an interested bystander to ask the minister's ruling on the social priority for the welfare of camels. This is a far-out example of what may happen when the work of a public official is regarded, by those in political authority over him and by his own estimate of the job, as merely the technical organization of political wishes. There are many circumstances which impose this restraint on the administrator.

In those government systems where large numbers of public officials move in and out of office with changes in political fortunes, the administrator has little choice but to be committed, uncritically, to prevailing political purposes. Insecurity of tenure and low wages often impel him to seek other sources of income than his government post offers. It is not uncommon to find such an official holding one or two other regular jobs while employed in public service. In such circumstances the administrator may not have the concern, the time nor the opportunity to see his work as an effective aid to national development. Administrative reforms, new methods of public administration training, and a heightened social awareness of the organizational requirements for effective national development are producing gradual improvements in many public administration systems. Much remains in both the attitudes of public administrators and in the nature of public administration structures that vitiates the declared purposes of social development.

If the administrator sees his function as something wider than carrying out political orders, what is it and what are the conditions for fulfilling it?

For most developing countries the attainment of independence from former colonial rule, and the subsequent establishment of formal development plans, have made imperative a fresh look at their traditional public administration systems. Administrative structures that served the purposes of imperial hegemonies must be reappraised in the light of national independence. Administrative tasks for the fulfilment of national plans will often be different, and certainly more specialized, than hitherto. The senior administrator particularly will have a vital responsibility for suggesting new organizational structures and administrative techniques appropriate to national development planning. While later publications have extended and made more explicit its substance, the United Nations Handbook on Public Administration (U.N., 1961) remains an excellent guide to some fundamental issues for public administration in developing countries.

If administration in the new states is to suffer a sea-change, men and women must be trained to understand why and how it is to be given re-direction. It is not so long since colonial 'masters' thought it their duty to train local 'bushmen' in the refinements of civilized behaviour. Within administrative training units, in addition to classroom work on administrative law, this often meant an early morning canter on your favourite grey (never a 'white'), the growth of dexterity in handling cake forks and manipulating tea-time chatter, the acquisition of a panoply of social skills and social attitudes germane to the society (or at least one section of it) from which the masters emerged. However initially he may lean on the experience of international consultants, the local administrator has the responsibility to recommend what kinds of people should be prepared for what variety of new administrative duties and what types of training programmes are best suited to these purposes. The United Nations has recently issued the results of its survey (U.N., 1966) on Public Administration Training Programmes in each region of the world.

Whatever the administrative text-books may suggest, there is no indisputable dividing line between the policy decisions made by the politician and the administrative decisions made by the public official. One writer (Sampson, 1962) with an extensive knowledge of British government practices has suggested that with the advent of a new minister in a department, a settling down period of from three to six weeks establishes whether the minister is to run the department or vice versa. In many a developing country where the life expectation of any government can be very short, and where ministers come and go with great frequency, the only continuous element of government, other than the courts, may be the public official. Under these conditions, even if he is not determining political policy, it is true enough to say of the administrator that he is making decisions and giving direction to departmental work that in other circumstances would be considered the responsibility of political leadership. The reverse process, of course, happens often enough when politicians seek to control an administrative system that appears inimical to the direct expression of their political purposes. In some countries an interesting hybrid is found in posts that carry both political authority and administrative responsibilities.

From these three possible areas of administrative responsibility what can we suggest about the function of the public official in developing countries? That he is the adviser to his political leader on the administrative feasibility of declared political aims? That he is one of the architects of administrative re-organization and new measures for administrative training? That he is capable in special situations of taking responsibility for a wide range of decisions not elsewhere required of the administrator? That he can don the Janus mask in looking to the demands of the politician and the requirements of the public interest? In other words that he is imaginative, flexible, and inventive as well as organizationally thorough? Regrettably, in some places, he displays few of these virtues, whether due to the stultifying effects of a particular political regime or to his own ineptitude. Where he is alive to the implications of the administrator's contribution to national development and is not hopelessly thwarted by forces of inertia or reaction, the administrator's role in social planning is as vital as any other component of development.

The national plan

The last two decades have witnessed the emergence in low

income countries of a major institution—The National Development Plan. Any satisfying definition of development planning would require an article in itself; perhaps here it is enough to say that it is concerned with the systematic application of knowledge and skills to the integrated development of existing resources or to the creation of new resources for the social and economic advancement of a whole population. National Plans, varying in time span and the scope of their objectives, are now the pace-setters for development in most impoverished countries. One of the most comprehensive statements about Plan Formulation and Execution is that given in a recent publication by Waterston (1965).

Plan characteristics

Is the Plan some magic formula discovered in the latter part of the twentieth century as a remedy for age-long poverty and stagnation? In low income countries has there been until recently no planning, no development? Certainly there has been both but current development programmes include objectives and techniques, which, if not entirely novel, represent in total a fresh approach to the endemic ills of poor nations. The most significant of these factors may be:

(i) The emphasis on time in plan programmes, which provides a focus of attention to what achievement is expected in a given period and allows a continuous appraisal of progress.

(ii) A more systematic and more comprehensive analysis of current and potential resources.

(iii) The direct application of external aid to a country's development objectives.

(iv) The re-organization of administrative structures and administrative procedures for planning purposes, involving changes at national, regional and local government levels.

(v) The education and training of people qualified to fulfil the specialized tasks of development programmes.

Plan deficiencies

All this and heaven too? National planning has shown uneven results from country to country and within the one country. Hanson's study of the Indian Development Plans (Hanson, 1966) is a perceptive account of gain and loss in a national planning programme. In some places, confidence has grown with achievement; elsewhere despondency has followed the failure to obtain even limited objectives. In our time, the obstacles to effective planning are formidable. As yet there are scant criteria by which the aims or the methods of planning can be assessed effectively. There are no reliable 'models' although some progress has been achieved in micro-analysis, drawing out, for example, the implications of experiences in experimental or demonstration farming.

A corollary to this lack of exact knowledge is the scarcity of people of authoritative experience in planning organization and techniques. Few there are in the planning field possessing a comparable expertise to that found in the medical, scientific and technological disciplines. Figures published by O.E.C.D. in 1966 indicated that of all the personnel advising governments on development planning, less than one per cent had taken any formal studies or training in that subject. One consequence is the large gap that often exists between the ideas of planning 'experts' and those who have to be responsible for executing the plans. One African country, aware of its huge reservoir of unexploited resources, established a bureau of economic planning in its largest central ministry and accepted the assistance of an international organization in the staffing of the bureau. The foreign consultants appointed issued a statement of intent so obscure and talked a technical language so incomprehensible that no local official was able to understand what the consultants were talking about or what was expected of him. The country's potential sources of wealth remained untapped while the professional insecurity of the experts and the inexperience of the officials sought a means of effective communication. Of course, it is not always thus but it happens often enough as a serious impediment to development planning.

In an earlier chapter reference was made to the paradoxical situation in developing countries where the human and material resources required for development can only be expected to exist in affluent societies. In the 1950's, one of the large Asian countries had but two qualified statisticians to assist government in the critical period of its first five year development plan. A university in this country sought the services of the statisticians for a brief lecturing assignment in courses on research methodology. With their numerous commitments in every part of the country the statisticians had to name a date eighteen months ahead during which time two groups of students had passed out of the university without any basis of statistical knowledge in their research training. Such situations are common in developing countries. The contribution of international consultants and increased professional training at home and abroad for local people is gradually producing more personnel with skills appropriate to the country's needs. In the Asian country mentioned above, there is no longer the same delay in answering a request for specialized services. In many other countries, however, there remains the sense of having to run to remain on the same spot. The growing awareness of what should be sought through national planning is not matched by the development of resources that can help to achieve it. By many, this is considered to be the most perplexing problem for developing countries.

Intermediate technology

A significant comment on this huge gap between needs and resources in development planning has been made by those advocating the greater use of intermediate technology in meeting the present requirements of impoverished countries. In their estimation, international technical assistance programmes which give support to rapid industrialization in low income countries arrest the development of the rural sector of the economy, concentrate work activity in swollen pockets of population in a few parts of the country, impose advanced technical processes on countries without the skills and the traditions to absorb them, increase dependence on foreign exchange for the purchase of sophisticated machinery and equipment, and do little to develop local initiative or improve employment potential. In contrast to all this, they suggest there is the need for simpler technologies which take account of the human resources available, the social environment in which new industries are to be introduced, and the size of the market for work output. There is good hope for development where the new technologies are within the range of a community's ability to absorb new ideas and techniques, and where they can be reproduced locally with local materials for local use, and cheaply enough to bring investment and market sales within the scope of local initiative. Those who stress the importance of intermediate technologies (*Tools for Progress*, 1968) insist that a national plan which fails to give full weight to this requirement of development will at many points be wasteful and irrelevant.

The purposes of a plan

A national plan is both an act of government and a response of a community, requiring the authority of the one to give it shape, the participation of the other to make it work. It can be a powerful instrument for defining and developing the resources required to grapple with the immensity of social need in a developing country. Plans go awry, or in fulfilment leave a sense of greater problems still unsolved, but among many peoples they can act as a stimulus to clarify and promote the fulfilment of their greatest social needs.

Research

Two main factors limit the scope of research work in

developing countries. First, the sheer scarcity of people trained and experienced in research methodology. Secondly, the conviction held by many influential leaders that research is very costly and rather esoteric in the dire circumstances that afflict their peoples. These two considerations are more closely linked than they might at first appear.

Scarcity of research

The dearth of people qualified to undertake research in developing countries is undeniable. Some governments have made strenuous efforts to equip a corps of specialists with this brand of expertise; even then they are often found becalmed in an administrative lagoon, removed from the main currents of national life. Other governments have enlisted the services of international consultants to advise them or engage directly on research activities. In many places the consultants' contributions in this way to the design of national planning have been vital, as has been their preparation of local people for research work. Withal, research work in some developing countries is minimal, spasmodic and in its nature often considered of peripheral value to what must be the main preoccupations of governments. The absolute shortage of funds for research must never be under-estimated, but an equally limiting factor is the concepts and attitudes about research held by those with authority to determine how far it should be encouraged. At the time of this writing, a senior official of a large African country visiting Britain stated forcefully to an academic audience his conviction that one of the greatest administrative deficiencies, if not the greatest, in present-day Africa, was its lack of qualified research workers. His plea was for training facilities in Britain which would offer his compatriots a thorough grounding in the knowledge of research methodology and statistics.

Some time ago an international agency circulated to governments and educational institutions in developing countries a five-page questionnaire seeking information about their research requirements, and systems and methods they would want to employ in prosecuting the research. One university department undertook a brief survey of the questionnaire itself and reached the conclusion that just to complete the form satisfactorily would require the services of two qualified research assistants for a period of nine months. The international agency was informed of this but perhaps considering it to be a frivolous or obstructive response, made no reply. Events of this kind confirm the prejudices of those who consider formal research too expensive, too elaborate, too 'academic' for the critical problems that confront them daily.

Research is vital to the purposes of social planning, to a proper understanding of how what is sought can be related to what exists, or can be expected to exist, in a determined period ahead. Manpower planning, economic investment, the determination of social priorities, the necessary reorganization of political and administrative activity; decisions about these and many other national requirements must be based on authoritative research. The alternative may be the squandering of slender resources on wasteful guesses about social need and the means to meet it. So far so good, as written down in this appraisal of requirements for effective national development. The carrying of this conviction to others demands more than a theoretical exposition of the value of research. Something like an intermediate technology in research training is required to demonstrate the vital place of research in national development. Often occurring, almost spontaneously, an unpretentious social enquiry has caught the imagination of those who would be the first to resist a proposal for a formal research project.

The beginnings of research

Some time ago a Community Development Programme in an Asian capital city set up an information centre in a locality of 10,000 people, most of them extremely poor and illiterate. The first 'customer' at the centre was a very old woman carrying a squawking hen refusing to lay eggs. What should she do with such a stubborn bird? The duty officer, an eager young man with a B.Litt. and currently a social work student, was nonplussed at this cry for help. After consultation with fellow workers he began a random enquiry in the neighbourhood which indicated a high incidence of barren poultry and gave him also some information about the food available to domestic hens. At a subsequent citizens' meeting, representatives of the area were encouraged to seek the advice of the Ministry of Agriculture, an unprecedented occasion for both them and the Ministry. After the initial bewilderment of such a confrontation, the Ministry agreed to detail one of its officials for an on-the-spot enquiry and to establish a continuing liaison with official representatives of the community. An important accompaniment to this activity was the interest shown by an expertly staffed Agricultural Research Centre which for two decades had been unable to effect any changes in the antiquated, wasteful farming methods universal in the rural areas surrounding it. The Centre's substantial research activity had resulted in producing no more than an oasis of demonstration crops, fruit trees and livestock, in the barren agricultural environment surrounding them. The most significant results of the Centre's work were utilized in some affluent countries but not until that time by the government or the people it was established to serve. For the Centre this creation of a bridge between community needs and available resources was an event of the first importance.

There can be no certainty about it because it was not tried, but it is highly probable that in the circumstances described above little success would have attended any proposal, from whatever source it originated, for a formal research programme on the care of domestic livestock. In this particular case, the confidence gained by local people from their encounter with the Ministry of Agriculture led to their appraisal of other community needs and the sources of help that might be available to them, within and outside their locality. The case of the recalcitrant chook led to a chain of enquiries that brought the first semblances of research into a community and provided ultimately a research programme which enlisted and trained even illiterate citizens as field workers in social surveys.

A young man at one time promised only a few months of survival over the ravages of tuberculosis listened to a public address in which a government medical officer directing the treatment of the disease outlined some harsh, but inescapable, realities for tuberculosis sufferers. In this populous country where over 60% of adults and children were afflicted, the doctors, clinics, drugs available, could reach only a fraction of the victims. Outlining the nature of the resources required for the treatment of T.B., particularly the need for domiciliary care, the medical officer was making the serious proposal that in the foreseeable future only those possessing a certain minimum family income should be given treatment. The rest must submit to the course of the disease. Any treatment policy less drastic than this merely dissipated the scarce facilities existing.

Whatever the logic of this argument in the circumstances of the country concerned, the medical officer's audience reacted in horrified alarm to the suggestion that tens of thousands of people should be turned away from hospitals and clinics to die. The young man, whose life had once hung by a thread with this ailment, could not accept the definitive conclusion of the medical officer. In the months that followed this meeting, he made exhaustive enquiries in a large neighbourhood of one city about the following issues: how many families believed one or more of their numbers to be suffering from tubercular ailments; what were the living conditions of these affected members and how, if at all, were they being medically treated; what did people know about the symptoms of the disease, the seriousness of it, and the treatment necessary to combat it; what would they be prepared to do in helping either their own family members or others who had contracted this illness.

In another set of enquiries, the young man approached private doctors, public health officials, commercial and industrial firms, international organizations, voluntary welfare agencies, university staff and students, to glean certain information: if the people of a neighbourhood were anxious to see a community programme launched to tackle the causes and effects of this insidious disease, and were themselves willing to participate in its planning and execution, what money, equipment, professional services, volunteer help and administrative support might be promised to assist community effort?

This was at least one success story. In a little under two years, the young man's careful enquiries began to bear fruit. With the help of public health officials, private donors, unpaid assistance from medical practitioners, volunteer services from a wide cross section of the society, and above all the active participation of the affected families, a number of treatment centres were opened which in addition to X-ray facilities provided simple medical advice on the treatment and care of T.B. Elementary training courses, designed for both volunteer workers and the affected families, provided simple information about domestic hygiene, invalid care, public health issues. The activity and the interest generated by this initiative attracted attention in other major centres of population where similar programmes were later introduced. The young man also edited a periodical dealing with the factors contributing to tuberculosis and with the types of treatment, simple and more elaborate, that should be the concern of health planners. This periodical was not only the first of its kind in the country; it was the only regular health publication known.

All the enthusiasm and hard work of such community organization to combat T.B. could achieve just so much; the eradication of the disease demanded the resources of national planning. The voluntary effort, by establishing facts and demonstrating achievements, gave hope to a society that a scourge fed of their poverty and ignorance was not invincible.

The dimensions of research

The last two illustrations are not intended to suggest that the organization of research in developing countries can be left to the inspired efforts of individuals and communities. National Planning is concerned with profound and complicated problems whose resolution demands, initially, thorough and expert investigation. At the same time, the success of research work will depend on local understanding of what it seeks to achieve. Again, the first initiative for research has often come from individuals and groups with no knowledge or experience of its techniques. It is regrettable that sometimes research consultants have failed to recognize these facts.

U.N.R.I.S.D.

A current research programme of fundamental importance to the definition of social policy in developing countries is being directed by the U.N. Research Institute for Social Development. The institute's official purpose is 'to conduct research into problems and policies of social development and economic development during different phases of economic growth'. This intention springs from the growing conviction that the largely economic emphasis in development policy and planning allows scant recognition of either the social determinants or the social consequences of development. A corollary to this is the need felt by social planners for more precise understanding of the relationship between social development and economic development.

The predominance of economic concepts in development planning is due, among other things, to the analytical tools available to economists. These tools are more precise in their measurement, and allow greater analytical skill, than anything available to the social planners. Social concepts are still relatively ambiguous; the quantification of social achievement is rudimentary and imprecise. While it is true that the development process is indivisible—it is an artificial distinction to talk of an economic process and of a social process—the aims and the consequences of development can be examined in either economic or social terms. What are these social and economic elements in development? How are they related to each other? What is meant by the reference to 'socio-economic reality'? What is the distinction between social capital and economic capital? To what extent can social concepts be quantified? Even if this is not always possible, is there any means of demonstrating the productivity effects of non-quantitative elements in development? How far is it possible to apply a system of cost-benefit analysis to social projects?

These are only a few of the questions with which the Research Institute for Social Development is concerned. In its work to date, part of it described in a number of stimulating reports (Research Institute, 1965-7), the Institute is demonstrating the essential role of social research in development planning. Tortuous decisions have to be made by planners in recommending to impoverished governments priorities for social expenditure. More refined analytical tools, a greater capacity to assess the validity of their concepts, could provide a touchstone for the social planner's growing confidence in his ability to measure and demonstrate the force of the social component in development.

Training

Perhaps enough has been said in earlier chapters about the quality and variety of training programmes required to prepare people for the tasks of social development. A wide range of training facilities is essential—at one extreme equipping social policy advisers with the detailed knowledge and the broad social perspective they must acquire if they are to grapple effectively with the problems of social planning; at the other extreme, providing voluntary social workers with sufficient elementary knowledge and skill to give their work a purposive direction. In the straitened circumstances of many countries, there may be too few resources to provide adequate training facilities at both of these extremes and for the types of training required between these extremes—for professional social workers, health visitors, community development workers, hospital administrators, probation officers, youth leaders, and for many others. Desirably, for the development of a number of complementary social services, training should be provided for all these categories of workers, and some countries are doing so. For many others, the cost is prohibitive.

Involved in the cost of training is the growing recognition that the organizers and instructors of training programmes must be furnished with more than the expertise of their particular disciplines: they must also be skilled in the use of training techniques. This is a recent conviction. In the past, in both affluent and impoverished countries, the teacher training colleges have been the notable example of programmes designed to instruct the instructor. In most other professional fields, teachers have been recruited primarily for their subject knowledge and seldom because of their demonstrated ability to teach. From his own experience, the reader will appreciate the lamentable results that often follow from this limited basis for selection of teaching staff in many educational institutions.

A recent innovation in training instruction has been the annual courses provided by the Royal Institute of Public Administration in Britain for training staff from developing countries. The courses, of four to five months' length, are planned for experienced public officials who in government training institutes, in universities, or in government departments, hold or are to assume organizational and teaching responsibilities in public administration training programmes. The curriculum seeks to make explicit both the educational purposes of public administration courses and the variety of techniques that can contribute to effective training. A major intention of these new training programmes is that the course members on their return home should be qualified to teach techniques of instruction and the methods of training course organization to the future staff of their training units. If this aim succeeds, there can be considerable savings in the choice and preparation of key training personnel to share their knowledge and experience with large numbers of teachers where training abroad would be too costly to consider. As the numbers of people trained abroad in this way grow, local training facilities for public administration teaching staff will make unnecessary the provision of such facilities abroad. This type of training could be of wide application for the requirements of developing countries, providing the expertise of instruction for personnel of varied professional disciplines. There may not always be the need to create special courses for the purpose. Existing professional training programmes might well give attention to a curriculum element that assists the student to an understanding of the methodology as well as the content of his training course.

Human resources

Most developing countries possess ample supplies of two major resources—land and people. The misuse of the first and the neglect of the second are characteristic features of many low income economies. Only in recent years has proper attention been given to the significance of 'human capital' in the assessment of potential national resources for the purposes of development planning. For many governments this has required a considerable mental and emotional leap. Often, plans have been considered the province of experts, planning the imposition of new or additional economic measures on a largely impoverished and illiterate society. That the members of that society, be they ever so humble, are vital sources of wealth; that planning, unless it is with people as well as for them, might be ultimately self-defeating—such simple facts have not always been obvious to those officials responsible for national planning programmes. The consequences have been shown in over-ambitious plans and in the failure to utilize effectively the human resources available for development purposes.

The O.E.C.D. 1967 Review of Development Assistance Efforts and Policies carries this reminder: 'It must be said again and again that economic development depends eventually upon the less developed countries themselves. It is their resources which will provide most of the necessary capital, their manpower which must be the source of labour, skilled and unskilled, and their institutions which must provide the basic framework for the new national objectives. The primary political decisions are theirs.' Why has something so obvious so often been overlooked?

Some of the reasons have been suggested earlier in this text: traditional attitudes of the élite to the unenlightened mass; the lack of social or political institutions that can effectively represent the opinions of citizens or utilize their capacities; the desire for rapid achievement where time and tide can wait for no man, least of all for the individuals, perhaps millions of them, whose reconditioning to the challenge of development seems an impossible task; the impact of international aid, frequently requiring a government to place the interests and convictions of a donor before their own preferred designs for social and economic development. On this last issue, a significant statement came recently from President Ayub of Pakistan, who, against the background of a developing system of basic democracies in his country, declared to the world at large that Pakistan wished to see its relationship with other countries as a relationship of friends, not one of dependence.

Many developing countries have hardly begun to tap the

potential resources of human intelligence and human skill that await realization within their own societies. In earlier chapters, attention has been drawn to some of the measures taken in many countries to encourage the development of unrealized abilities: community development programmes, intermediate technology schemes, literacy campaigns, training courses in elementary skills, the employment of professional aides, the establishment of a firm link between national planning proposals and the active response to them of people at every social and economic level. Social progress in these countries will be determined significantly by the wisdom and the ingenuity their governments display in harnessing the hitherto unexploited talents of their citizens to the purposes of development. It is as true as ever that to him that hath shall be given—if only he knows what he has.

7
Conclusion

In a developing country, the degree of social change that must anticipate and accompany new national planning may be given impetus by a variety of political measures. Violent or bloodless revolution has been effected through military intervention or by the rise to power of clandestine political movements. More rarely, the accession to office of a recognized political party with a radical platform has constituted a type of revolution. Elsewhere, for the present at least, countries are seeking to promote change through extensions and modifications of the traditional political and social structure. In the circumstances of either revolution or gradualism, the required changes in political, economic and social institutions, the measures for the development of material resources, the organization of effective social planning may be decided and directed by a minority élite or by a process that allows the significant participation of people of all levels of society. Again, the objective of early planning may be one of economic concentration on growth areas of wealth even if this policy has to neglect the immediate fortunes of a generation or two of some millions of citizens. Whether this be done, or an alternative plan pursued of distributing social benefits more widely at each stage of development, is likely to be determined by domestic vested interests and external political pressures as much as by an objective theory of effective development policy.

CONCLUSION

This present examination of social policy in developing countries has sought to emphasize those human needs and requirements for social change which confront any government and any people wherever their political and international affiliations lie, whatever their economic and social convictions may be. The ideological forces that shape a country's destiny; the sources of the power that gives a regime its birth and maintains its stability: such factors affect profoundly what people are considered to need and what should be done, and by whom, to meet that need. No two countries are similar in their definition of social purposes, and the measures required to fulfil them; but the 'people', for whom social planning in many different forms is designed, are astonishingly alike in what they demonstrate of basic human needs.

Further reading

I am grateful to Mr. Robert Leaper of the Social Science Courses, University of Swansea, for his helpful advice on the range of references included here.

GENERAL

Some of the most significant writing on social policy and social planning has emerged in the reports of the United Nations agencies. Many of these reports have been referred to in the chapter bibliographies of this text. The reader who wishes to maintain an acquaintance with the progress of social planning in developing countries should read at least the annual reports of many of these agencies—the World Health Organization, the Food and Agricultural Organization, the International Labour Office, the United Nations International Children's Emergency Fund, the United Nations Educational, Scientific and Cultural Organization—and those of the U.N. Department of Economic and Social Affairs. If time permits, some of the U.N. agencies' occasional headquarters and regional office reports on specific social issues should be consulted. The U.N. Institute of Social Research in Geneva would be another source of relevant publications. Lists of such publications can be found in the monthly Catalogue of Her Majesty's Stationary Office, in the Monthly Chronicle of the United Nations, or by request to a United Nations Information Office (their address in London is 14-15 Stratford Place, London, W.1.). Such lists will often provide information also about publications on the work of the Colombo Plan, the Organization for European Co-operation and Development, and other technical assistance agencies, multilateral and bilateral, outside the U.N. Although not always so readily procurable, the reports of National Foundations provide useful information on the dimensions of private assistance to social development in low income countries.

Independent author publications in this subject are not numerous. An increasing number of articles is to be found in a variety of journals and periodicals but for the general reader they may not be easy to track down. Among the larger works, J. Arthur Lewis, *The Theory of Economic Growth* (Allen and Unwin, 1955) remains one of the most stimulating analyses of the social concomitants of national development. A recent publication analysing the successes and failures of social scientists in economic development is *A Re-Appraisal of Economic Development*, edited by Whiteford (Aldine Publishing Company, Chicago, 1967). A further reference to note is *Social Aspects of Economic Development* by Chester L. Hunt (McGraw Hill, New York and London, 1966). U.N.E.S.C.O. (1963) has issued a two volume report on the same theme entitled *Social Aspects of Economic Development in Latin America*. For many specific examples of the social factors in development, the reader should consult *A Casebook of Social Change*, edited by Arthur H. Niehoff (Aldine Publishing Company, Chicago, 1966), which presents evaluations of attempts to introduce change in the five major developing areas of the world. Although focused on the British scene, T. H. Marshall's *Social Policy*, (Hutchinson, London, 1965), raises many issues pertinent to the social development of low income countries.

On world population issues, a mass of official statistical information and of non-official writings makes difficult any assessment of priorities in further reading. The short simple statement found in the 1966 U.N. publication *World Population: Challenge to Development*, provides a stimulating beginning for a possible wider interest in demographic problems. Attention should be given to the reports of the Population Division of the Department of Economic and Social Affairs, United Nations Secretariat, New York.

EDUCATION

Education Policy, Educational Planning and Educational Administration

In addition to the works of Hunter and Curle, reference should be made to the publications of the International Institute for Educational Planning, address 7 rue Eugene Delacroix, Paris 16e. Their most important publications to date are: *Educational Planning: A Bibliography*, 1964; *Educational Planning: An Inventory of Major Research Needs*, 1965; *Educational Planning: a Directory of Training and Research Institutions*, 1964; *Problems and Strategies of Educational Planning: Lessons from Latin America*, 1965; *African Research Monographs; New Educational Media in Action: Case Studies for Planners*, 1967 (three volumes); *The New Media: Memo to Educational Planners*, by W. Schramm, P. H. Coombs, F. Kahnert, J. Lyle; and their six publications in the series, 'Fundamentals of Educational Planning'. A publication of O.E.C.D., 2 rue Andre Pascal, Paris 16e, *Organizational Problems in Planning Educational Development*, deals with many of the issues examined in this book.

Literacy

U.N.E.S.C.O. has become the key agency for information and analysis of literacy needs and literacy programmes. A reader's special interest in this problem might be met by acquiring a list of publications on this subject direct from U.N.E.S.C.O. in Paris. A brief exposition of the problem is found in *A.B.C. of Literacy*, M. Burnet (U.N.E.S.C.O., 1965).

Manpower

Written material on the relationship of manpower estimates and educational planning is growing fast. Three works might be consulted: *Manpower Forecasting in Educational Planning* (O.E.C.D., 1967); Harbison and Myers, *Education, Manpower and Economic Growth* (McGraw Hill, New York and London, 1964); Harbison and Myers, *Manpower and Education (Country Studies in Economic Development)* (McGraw Hill, New York and London, 1965.)

HEALTH

Apart from the publications of the World Health Organization in Geneva, which continues to be the main source of our knowledge on health issues in developing countries, most writings on health planning and health administration are to be found in books or reports which examine a wide expanse of need in less developed nations. Reference has already been made to such writings in the chapter bibliographies.

Described by one reviewer as an essay in medico-social philosophy, Rene Dubos' *Mirage of Health* (Allen and Unwin, London, 1960), is a very different type of statement about human disease than is usually found in publications on international health. For the range of issues which include public health and health education, community organization for health, rural health services, mental health, hospital facilities, nutrition, medical research, and doctor and medical auxiliary training, the reader would be well advised to begin with a book already mentioned, *Medical Care in Developing Countries*, edited by Maurice King (Oxford University Press, London, 1966). The comprehensive bibliography at the back of this book is an excellent guide for further reading in this subject.

SOCIAL WELFARE

Children

Among the many publications of U.N.I.C.E.F., reference should be made to a report, *Planning for the Needs of*

Children in Developing Countries, edited by Herman D. Stein (U.N.I.C.E.F., 1964).

The Delinquent and the Disabled

Delinquent problems and programmes are examined in some of the publications already mentioned above. Further material is available from the U.N. Division of Social Defence, New York. For many issues concerned with measures for the disabled, the publications of the International Labour Office in Geneva are relevant.

Community Development and Community Effort for Social Welfare

A sizeable literature does exist and choices for priority reading are difficult to make. At the least, one should look at *Community Development and National Development*, U.N. Department of Economic and Social Affairs (New York, 1963); *Community Development and Economic Development*, two parts (U.N. Economic Commission for Asia and the Far East, Bangkok, 1960); *Inducing Social Change in Developing Communities* (U.N. Research Institute for Social Development, 1967, Sales No. 67,IV,4); *Communities and their Development*, by T. R. Batten (Oxford University Press, London, 1957); *The Organisation of a Community Development Programme*, by P. du Sautoy (Oxford University Press, London, 1962). An important periodical is the *Community Development Journal*, published quarterly by: The Editor, 22 Kingston Road, Didsbury, Manchester, 20, U.K.

DETERMINANTS OF SOCIAL POLICY

Economic

He would be a brave man indeed who was prepared to recommend any one book from the wealth of literature available in this field. Lewis' *Theory of Economic Growth* is a more than adequate starting point. One might then continue with: J. Bhagwati, *The Economics of Underdeveloped Countries* (Weidenfeld and Nicolson, London,

1966); R. Theobald, *The Rich and the Poor* (New English Library, London, 1966); M. Dobb, *Economic Growth and Underdeveloped Countries* (Lawrence & Wishart, London, 1963); A. Shonfield, *The Attack on World Poverty* (Chatto & Windus, London, 1960), and H. Myint, *The Economies of the Developing Countries* (Hutchinson, London, 1964).

Political

Two books have attracted particular interest: *The Politics of the Developing Areas*, Almond and Coleman (Princeton University Press, 1960); and *The Man on Horseback*, S. E. Finer (Pall Mall Press, London, 1962). But these are only two of many.

Cultural (Tradition and Change)

The writings of Margaret Meade have made a large reading audience aware of the significance of social values and cultural traditions in any estimate of the roles that people may play in national development. Two other authors are worth noting here: Lucy Mair, particularly her *New Nations* (Weidenfeld and Nicolson, London, 1963); and J. G. Peristiany, in his editorship of *Honour and Shame. The Values of Mediterranean Society* (Weidenfeld and Nicolson, London, 1965).

The Family and the Role of Women

Some of the most important references are contained in certain of the reports already mentioned. Further brief but pertinent comment on these subjects is to be found in the report of the U.N. Conference on the Application of Science and Technology for the Benefit of the Less Developed Areas, particularly *Volume V: People and Living* (U.N., New York, 1963).

Aid

Most technical assistance programmes, whether multilateral or bilateral, publish reports on both the purpose and the scope of their aid. On many general issues concerned with the giving of aid, the publications of The Overseas Development Institute Ltd., 160 Piccadilly, London, W.1. are particularly relevant. The most comprehensive, which examines the national aid programmes of the four major western donors, United States, France, Britain, and Germany, is *Effective Aid* (O.D.I., London, 1967).

THE INSTRUMENTS OF SOCIAL POLICY

Legislation

In addition to the works already mentioned of Lee, and Burns (Ed.), the reader might consult the relevant chapters of *The Approach to Self-Government,* by Sir Ivor Jennings (Cambridge University Press, 1956).

Administration

Among the numerous publications available, an effective background work to the subject of administration in developing countries is *A Handbook of Public Administration* (U.N. New York, Sales No. 61.II.H2). Much has been written on the subject since, both by the U.N. and others, but the handbook remains a stimulating appraisal of the issues with which politicians, administrators and political scientists have to be concerned. Another relevant reference is *The Civil Service in New African States,* by A. L. Adu (Allen & Unwin, London, 1965).

National Planning

Again, a wealth of material available. For a comprehensive statement on the range of issues within the subject, see *Development Planning. Lessons of Experience,* by Albert Waterston (Johns Hopkins Press, 1965).

Intermediate Technology

In addition to the writings of the Group of this name, a helpful bibliography has been published under the title *Technology for Underdeveloped Areas,* by Baranson (Pergamon Press, London, 1967).

FURTHER READING

Research

The 1955 publication of the Food and Agricultural Organization (Via delle Terme di Caracalla, 00100—Rome), *Fact-Finding with Rural People*, remains one of the most stimulating accounts of the role of research in developing countries.

Training

Particularly appropriate to some of the themes in this book are the U.N. International Surveys of Training for Social Work. The fourth Survey, Sales No. 65.IV.3, raises many important questions for future consideration.

Human Resources

Again, the U.N. Report, *Science and Technology for Development*, particularly *Volume V, People and Living*, and *Volume VI, Education and Training*, has immediate relevance. And, *Human Problems in Technological Change*, edited E. H. Spicer (Russell Sage Foundation, New York, 1952).

Bibliography

A.I.D. (1966) *A.I.D. Participant Training Program—An Evaluation Study*, U.S. Department of State, A.T.D., Washington, D.C.

BAILEY, F. G. (1966) 'The Peasant View of the Bad Life', *The Advancement of Science*, Vol. 23, No. 14, December 1966, School of African and Asian Studies and Institute of Development Studies, University of Sussex.

BALOGH, THOMAS (1965) 'Land Tenure, Education and Development in Latin America', *Problems and Strategies of Educational Planning. Lessons from Latin America*, UNESCO, International Institute for Educational Planning.

BURNS, SIR ALAN, ed. (1966), *Parliament as Export*, Allen & Unwin, London.

F.A.O. (1966) *State of Food and Agriculture.*

FINER, S. E. (1962) *The Man on Horseback*, Pall Mall Press, London.

HANSON, A. H. (1966) *The Process of Planning—A Study of India's Five Year Plans, 1950-64*, Oxford University Press, London.

Human and Social Impact of Technological Change in Pakistan (1956). A report on a survey conducted by the University of Dacca, East Pakistan, and published with the assistance of UNESCO (2 vols.), Oxford University Press, London.

KING, MAURICE (1966) *Medical Care in Developing Countries. A primer on the Medicine of Poverty*, Oxford University Press, London.

LAMBE, JAMES, ed. (1967) *Rich World/Poor World*, Arrow Books, London.

LEE, J. M. (1967) *Colonial Development and Good Government*, Allen & Unwin, London.

MOYES, ADRIAN, and HAYTER, TERESA (1964) *World III, a handbook on developing countries*, Overseas Development Institute, Pergamon Press, London.

RESEARCH INSTITUTE FOR SOCIAL DEVELOPMENT (1965-7) Reports:
1. *Aspects of Social and Economic Growth* (1965)
2. *Methods to induce change at the local level* (1965)
3. *Social and economic factors in development* (1966)
4. *The level of living index* (1966)
5. *Land tenure, land concentration and agricultural output* (1966)
6. *The social thresholds: patterns associated with economic growth* (1967)
7. *Cost-benefit analysis of social projects* (1966)
U.N., New York.

SAMPSON, ANTHONY (1962) *Anatomy of Britain*, Hodder & Stoughton, London.

Sunday Times (1967) 'Turning Waste to Food', Article on Nutrition, by Tony Clifton, 10 December 1967.

Tools for Progress 1967-8 (1968) Guide to Equipment and materials for small-scale development, The Inter-Technology Development Group, London.

U.N. (1954) *Some problems in the Organisation and Administration of Public Enterprise in the Industrial Field*, U.N., New York (Sales no. 1954,ii,H1).

U.N. (1958) *Management of Industrial Enterprises in Underdeveloped countries*, U.N., New York (Sales no. 58,ii,B5).

U.N. (1961) *A handbook on public administration*, U.N., New York (Sales no. 61.ii.H2).

U.N. (1963) *Report on the World Social Situation*, U.N., New York (Sales no. 63.iv.4).

U.N. (1966) *Handbook on Training in the Public Services*, U.N., New York (Sales no. 66.ii.H1).

UNESCO (1967) *World Illiteracy at mid-century: a statistical study.* Monographs on Fundamental Education, UNESCO, Paris.

WATERSTON, ALBERT (1965) *Development Planning—Lessons of Experience*, published for International Bank of Reconstruction and Development, Johns Hopkins Press, Baltimore.

WOOTTON, BARBARA (1959) *Social Science and Social Pathology*, Allen & Unwin, London.

WHO, (1967) *The work of WHO, 1966*, WHO, Geneva, March, 1967.

World of Opportunity (1963) Science and Technology for Development, U.N., New York.
1. World of Opportunity
2. Natural Resources
3. Agriculture
4. Industry
5. People and Living
6. Education and Training
7. Science and Planning
8. Plenary Procedure

For Product Safety Concerns and Information please contact our EU representative GPSR@taylorandfrancis.com
Taylor & Francis Verlag GmbH, Kaufingerstraße 24, 80331 München, Germany

www.ingramcontent.com/pod-product-compliance
Ingram Content Group UK Ltd.
Pitfield, Milton Keynes, MK11 3LW, UK
UKHW022122190926
475702UK00013B/1590

* 9 7 8 0 4 1 5 8 5 0 7 4 2 *